ISBN-13: 978-1497456044

ISBN-10: 1497456045

Dedication

This book is dedicated to all you Mama Grizzlies and Bad-ass Mothers who first sensed the danger posed by the cult of Common Core to our kids. You refused to retreat, you refused to be quiet, and you continue to fearlessly fight to protect our children and our country. You are an inspiration!

Table of Contents

Preface

"Knowledge will forever govern ignorance; and people who mean to be their own governors must arm themselves with the power which knowledge gives." James Madison

Americans must reclaim sovereignty over our children's education and minds. Governors across the country willingly handed over their state's control of education to the cult of Common Core for 30 pieces of silver offered by the Obama Administration in exchange for changing their state's education policies in 2010.

This book is my open letter to parents, teachers, and concerned citizens alike explaining my first-hand account of the cult of Common Core as I have experienced it as an insider, working on the Common Core test, and as a teacher who is feeling its impact on the children in my classroom. I explain what the Common Core is and where it may be heading, in plain, easy-to- read, and mostly acronym free language while there is still time to change its course of taking over our children's minds and evaporating our country's exceptionalism. I have made a concerted effort to keep this book as concise as possible so it may serve as a foundation in your own fight against the Common Core leviathan.

Calling the Common Core a "cult" is not an exaggeration. It is much bigger than just a set of standards, a test, or a data gathering machine. I thought about calling it a virus. Like a virus, the Common Core tricks its victims into lowering their guard by pretending to be something it is not. But the Common Core isn't just a mindless infection of our society; rather it is an intentional takeover of our education delivery system and therefore a takeover of our children's minds. It is antithetical to everything that makes our country exceptional. This cult is relentlessly pulling our children under its control, with a seemingly endless supply of money, and uses intimidation to silence its opponents.

My knowledge of the cult of Common Core is informed by my ten years of teaching in public schools, my five years working on state standardized tests, my participation in committees reviewing the Common Core/PARCC test, and my 48 years as an American who is very concerned about the implications for the fundamental transformation of our children's minds via the cult of Common Core.

Just as we are moving from theory to implementation with Obamacare and discovering that many politicians lied to us about its true nature, so too shall America begin discovering the true nature of the Common Core, and the motives of those who advocate for it, as it moves from theory to implementation in the upcoming year. But something funny happened on the way to Common Core's coronation. Parents, educators, and other grassroots groups started raising their voices to stop it.

Introduction

The plain truth is while you were busy working, playing, parenting, dealing with health issues, mid-life crises, being told you could keep your health care as you lost your health care, as you watched your house value go underwater, as you watched the news about the *IRS* targeting, gun running, *NSA* snooping, as you watched yet another child pop idol crash and burn, as you were keeping ahead of the wave of life, control over your children's minds has been in the crosshairs of a sucking, slithering, tentacled, leviathan.

If you ask a teacher, it is the newest same-old-thing-with-another-name program they are being forced to implement after taking umpteen workshops in an effort to decode it. They are just waiting for the test to come out so they can see what they should be teaching to.

If you ask a politician who mindlessly voted it into your life they will use the supplied talking points of "more rigorous", "critical thinking", "internationally benchmarked", and "college and career ready".

If you ask a student they will mention the odd, nonsensical math problems they are being asked to figure out using their brand new "aligned" textbooks their school district just bought for the quick fix.

If you ask a Progressive (Republican or Democrat) they may tell you in a rare moment of honesty that they are at long last within reach of one of their most prized goals that they have been salivating over for decades.

It is like the scene from the Stephen King novel-turned-movie, *It*, where the yellow-eyed clown appears from the dark recesses of a storm drain and tries to coax little Georgie to come closer to the storm drain opening to retrieve his lost paper boat, which the clown holds just out of reach. Georgie hesitates and ignores his gut instinct to run for his life and reaches instead for his beloved paper boat.

It is then that the clown's voice changes. His yellow fanged snarl reveals what Georgie's gut instinct told him was the truth all along, hidden beneath the cheery painted-on facade of the evil clown's face. His arm is clamped down upon by the clown's razor sharp claws in a death grip.

Before we know it little Georgie is pulled screaming, legs kicking, down into the abyss of the dark, dank storm drain. Add to that visual little Georgie's parents being pulled into the drain, followed by his teachers, his school, his school district, his state department of education, and his country's exceptionalism. Now you are starting to get the picture of the insidious education delivery system, the Common Core, metastasizing at a school near you.

1

My Little Georgie Moment

"If ever you find yourself environed with difficulties and perplexing circumstances, out of which you are at a loss how to extricate yourself, do what is right, and be assured that that will extricate you the best out of the worst situations."   **Thomas Jefferson**

If I had read the description of the Common Core in this book's "Introduction" a year ago I might have thought that it was a bit melodramatic. But as a teacher who has worked on the Common Core test I don't think the description goes far enough. After the first of three days working on the Common Core test in Chicago, in March of 2013, things just did not seem right.

I was asked by *the Arizona Department of Education* to fly to Chicago and work on the Common Core test, known as the *PARCC* test. Our state had just started the implementation of the Common Core standards so I wanted to understand them better. What were the standards? Who wrote them? Who approved them? What would the test look like? Who was running the show? I just wanted some clarity, and perhaps insight, so that I could adjust my teaching to help my students meet the new standards and share my knowledge with fellow educators who were just as in the dark as I was.

My eye-rolling Common Core handlers were not interested in my curiosity or all my enthusiastic questions. I was told that I was in Chicago to give feedback on the Common Core test and that I should check out the Common Core website to answer any questions that I had. Until then do not critique the test, the standards, or ask a litany of questions about where the standards came from or who wrote them.

Their attitude was as cold as the near zero temperatures outside our conference room window. I felt as if I was in some sort of cult that everyone else bought into bleary-eyed and I was the only one who was not with the program. I had not drunk the Common Core Kool Aid yet. Besides, I didn't speak in acronyms or talking points like the other higher level inductees of the cult of Common Core.

I am a quick learner though and got the message loud and clear. I kept my mouth shut and paid attention. My Common Core handlers' demeanor caused me to become suspicious that there was something else going on and things were not quite as they seemed. I was little Georgie standing outside the storm drain wanting to believe the best, but my gut instinct told me that something was very wrong.

Unlike with Georgie in my earlier analogy, my handlers showed me their fanged toothed snarl before I got close enough to get grabbed and pulled into the Common Core storm drain. In answer to questions I had about a student writing sample, my Common Core handler blurted out, "We don't ever care what the kids' opinions are. If they write what they think or put forth their opinion then they will fail the test."

I have always taught my students to think for themselves. They are to study multiple views on a given topic, then take their own position and support it with evidence. "That is the old way of writing, "my Common Core handler sighed. "We want students to repeat the opinions of the 'experts' that we expose them to on the test. This is the 'new' way of writing with the Common Core."

I discovered later that this was not just some irritated, rogue Common Core handler, rather this was a philosophy I heard repeated again and again. I pointed out that this was not the way that teachers teach in the classroom. She retorted that, "We expect that when the test comes out the teachers in the classroom will imitate the skills emphasized on the test (teach to the test) and employ this new way of writing and thinking."

I began to feel sick. What had I gotten myself into? This new way of thinking was to make our students into little brainwashed automatons that will just spew back a position on any topic given to them? Was I unwittingly playing a part in this scheme? Would other teachers really teach this "new" Common Core way?

Then I remembered that the Common Core method of evaluating teacher effectiveness ties teacher pay and teacher evaluations to student test scores. The new data systems under Common Core would enable central command to see what you are teaching in the classroom with online lesson plans, grade books, student grades, online textbooks and test scores. You bet your ass many teachers will adjust their teaching.

The Common Core master planners could decide that global warming is man caused in the articles presented on the test. Kids better repeat that belief in their essays or they will fail. If students fail, teachers will be held accountable financially and professionally. Therefore many teachers, being the good government bureaucrats they are, will teach to the test and ensure that kids learn not to think for themselves again. The truly good teachers with a conscience will either retire or change professions.

I began to imagine an administration coming to power that uses centrally controlled education to pour their political position, rather than factual content with multiple views, into the country's education system through federally approved and aligned textbooks. Teacher's online gradebooks and lesson plans would be monitored to ensure compliance with the administration's positions in science and history. Kids who dared to have their own viewpoint rather than repeating the "experts" in the textbooks would be punished academically to be more in line with an administration's views. On-line textbooks could also be instantly updated to reflect whatever the current political talking points are.

I began to do research into the Common Core and discovered a burgeoning resistance forming against it. Some groups decried the centralization of education and the loss of state and local sovereignty. Others complained about the ridiculous nature of the Common Core math questions, and others were suspicious of the biased political nature of the reading content they were seeing in Common Core aligned lessons and suggested readings.

There were those who were furious over NSA-like student data collection without parent permission being initiated by the Common Core, violating the spirit of education privacy laws. Some were suspicious of the groups that actually wrote the Common Core standards and decried the lack of transparency from those same groups that were not subject to Freedom of Information (FOIA) requests.

There were groups that were suspicious about the approval heaped on the Common Core by many in corporate America. Many others were grumbling about how quickly the Common Core was adopted by most state governors in cash strapped states with little or no public discussion or votes in state legislatures.

Surprisingly, the resistance to the Common Core was bipartisan with both the Left and the Right opposing them, albeit for different reasons. The support for the Common Core among moneyed establishment Progressives, both Republican and Democrat, was also bipartisan. Most people, teachers included, were too busy dealing with their lives so they were blissfully unaware of the Common Core structures being put in place to control the delivery of education.

2

The Obamacare of Education

"Masses come over to the side of the reform. Resistance is left to the minority, and such as will not be convinced are crushed." Woodrow Wilson, Progressive-in-Chief

The more rabbit holes I delved into, the more I had to broaden my concept of this leviathan called the Common Core. Just like when you look up an address on *MapQuest* and you have to keep zooming out for perspective and context with which to be able to understand where the location you are viewing is truly located, I had to keep zooming out with each new morsel of information to understand this Common Core thing.

What I discovered was disturbing. The Common Core is more than just new national teaching standards. It is more than a new national test that all our kids will be taking. It is more than the data suctioning systems that each state has now installed to suction all sorts of information into the Common Core machine's central command center. Common Core is the Obamacare of education.

Like Obamacare, the Common Core:

1. Was hurriedly written in secret with little to no input from the public.

2. Keeps its true goals camouflaged.
3. Is a federal government overreach into our lives in contradiction of clearly stated powers assigned to the states in the U.S. Constitution.
4. Is a federal and corporate intrusion into our private property (data).
5. Will lower the standards in a sector of society that it purports to want to raise.
6. Will cost much greater than promised.
7. Will add to the deterioration of our country's exceptionalism.
8. Was put into place by coercing states with the promise of federal money.
9. Is a collusion between Big Business hungering for profit and Big Government hungering for power and control.
10. Is a centrally controlled delivery system, shaped by Big Government and steeped in the Progressive world view of uniformity.
11. Is being opposed by a grassroots opposition as the effects of its implementation are being felt.

I use the term "Progressive" to mean those who would like to progressively move our country towards a centrally controlled model of governance overseen by a class of technocrats who know so much better how we should all live our lives. Progressives have infected both the Republican and Democratic parties whether their names are Bush or Obama.

Progressive philosophies have always been ultimately rejected by the American electorate when their true objectives have been exposed. So Progressives sunk down into the bureaucracies of federal agencies where real power could be exerted through regulations from the "bottom up" until they had administrations, both Republican and Democrat, who could exert power from the "top down". With the new Obama administration, coupled with the economic crash of 2008, Progressives had the perfect storm for education reform. They never let a good crisis go to waste.

American Progressivism is a world view irrespective of national boundaries. Ever wonder why they look to the rest of the world for models of how the United States should behave rather than espousing American exceptionalism and blazing our own trail? "Why can't our student test scores be just as high as Finland or South Korea?" you may have heard them shout. I honestly would like to shout back, "When Finland and South Korea achieve Google, EBay, Apple, a man on the moon, and the most powerful, advanced military in the world, then we'll discuss being more like them!"

What better way to slowly, progressively change the country's mindset then to have control over our children's minds by having full control of our education system? Progressives have already infiltrated our school systems with revisionist history and pseudoscience. The Common Core is just the final phase of their control. Wouldn't it be nice to just have one national/world mindset and stop having to deal with all these pesky states and localities pushing the individualism thing with differing political views and mindsets? Wouldn't it also be better to shape citizens who are functioning little worker bees, rather than informed citizens who strive toward the ideals of individuality and liberty that have made our country exceptional? This worked so well in Eastern Europe and the Soviet Union, for a time anyway.

As I continued to follow the Common Core leviathan I collected quite the list of acronyms like the NGA, OWG, CCSI, EBSR, TECR, CCSSO, CLG, SBAC, and PARCC to name a few. Every bloated government bureaucracy has their own language of acronyms to hide behind. The cult of Common Core is no exception and it brings another fifty shades of bureaucracy to an already bureaucracy-bloated education system.

The same names kept appearing time and time again as well. Besides Uncle Sam, the Common Core's most well-known sugar daddy is Bill Gates. Anytime a Common Core related group needs funding the Bill and Melinda Gates Foundation seems to open their purse.

When I returned back to school and began talking to other teachers I was amazed with how little they knew about the Common Core in general and about the growing opposition to it in particular. Most teachers just knew that they were mandated to participate in Common Core professional development at school to aid in comprehending the somewhat vague and often incomprehensible nature of the standards. They did not have time to see the bigger picture and in many cases were too busy with work and school to delve in further.

Like Obamacare, no one can escape the Common Core. Public, charter, private, and home school kids are all fair game. One of the architects of the Common Core, David Coleman, now the head of the College Board, is already pulling college admission tests and standards into the cult of Common Core. He is also dumbing down the SAT to make the college admission test more "accessible" making sure that all those dumbed downed Common Core indoctrinated kids can pass it. Test takers will no longer be penalized for wrong answers, encouraging guessing, and the essay portion of the test is now optional. That way they can get into college and start accumulating all that student debt with student loans that Uncle Sam now controls.

Mothers who have spoken out against the Common Core have been branded "white suburban moms" who are upset that their kids are not as brilliant as they thought they were, by the U.S. Secretary of Education, Arne Duncan. Remember when those who opposed Obamacare were called racists? Big Government does not like it when you challenge their takeovers.

Some states are even changing the name of the Common Core in their state to blunt criticism and obscure its identity. Big Government likes to play the name change game. In my state of Arizona they renamed the standards the *Arizona College and Career Ready Standards*. They can put lipstick on that pig, but it's still the federal government's bacon. Teachers advocating *against* the

Common Core, and the position of their state secretary of education or governor, fear they may face retribution.

There are new front groups being formed every day with Common Core money to push for its acceptance. Many groups, like the US Chamber of Commerce, push the idea that businesses just want a more educated work force while simultaneously pushing for amnesty to let unskilled, cheap labor flood into the country.

Other groups push the idea that colleges are enrolling kids that need much academic remediation due to the low standards of the public school system. How do these kids get into college if they need so much remediation? Are colleges that desperate for government backed student loan money that they lower their admission requirements?

Like Obamacare, the Common Core has recruited its own actors to push its acceptance. You may have seen these glassy-eyed teachers on television commercials lately saying how great the Common Core is. Teachers of the Year programs are also being used as the cult of Common Core's propagandists. Each state's "teacher of the year" is given cash, gifts, and speech training before fanning out across the country making the case for the Common Core. They fail to disclose that the National Teacher of the Year organization is a project of the CCSSO (Council of Chief State School Officers) which wrote the Common Core Standards and holds its copyright. Think anyone will ever be chosen as a teacher of the year by their interview committees if they profess a love for states' rights over education and oppose the Common Core?

Bill Gates is also funding the training of teachers to advocate on behalf of the Common Core before school boards and legislators. With money from the Gates Foundation he created a program called Teacher Voices Convening (TVC) to advocate on behalf of the cult of Common Core.

I decided to continue investigating this Common Core leviathan, following it wherever it might take me until this uncomfortable "something's wrong" feeling was either justified or disappeared.

3

From Where Did the Cult Spawn?

"Whoever would effect change in modern constitutional government must first educate his fellow citizens to want some change. That done he must persuade them to want the particular change he wants." Woodrow Wilson, Progressive-in-Chief

Before the cult of Common Core came along, each state created its own academic standards that spelled out what every child should know by the end of each grade level. Each state also created its own state test to assess whether its students learned what they were supposed to be learning at each grade level. The states had ownership and complete control of their standards and tests.

The U.S. Constitution guarantees that the states have sovereignty over educating their children and there is even federal law forbidding the setting up of a national curriculum. This is why the Common Core cultists robotically repeat the mantra that the federal government is not mandating a curriculum, because it is illegal.

It was not a perfect system, but which one is? America had a decentralized approach to education while also having national tests, like the NAEP (National Assessment of Educational Progress) and the Stanford Test, with which we could compare our students' progress nationally across state lines. Each state operated as a laboratory to test out different ways of educating children with states copying best practices of excelling states in many instances.

In Massachusetts, for instance, Dr. Sandra Stotsky set up the gold standard for language arts (reading and writing) standards along with assessments that showed huge gains in student learning. Many states then mimicked components of the Massachusetts standards in their own academic standards in a way that worked for their state's children.

America has an incredibly diverse population and this requires a diverse, *decentralized* approach to education. Let homogenized Finland and South Korea also have homogenized, one-size-fits-all education systems that produce professional test takers. Our kids are too busy changing the world.

Then along came the Great Recession of 2008. State coffers began drying up and education departments were eyed for cost saving cutbacks. In walked the Obama administration with a big bag of Stimulus money ($4.3 billion) in 2009. Remember the Stimulus money? It was supposed to be for shovel-ready-jobs, infrastructure, and to save teacher jobs? Along with the $4.3 billion carrot, came the stick of a new centralized vision for reforming education in the country to be headed by many of the same people who worked with State Senator Obama in the Chicago Public School System several years earlier.

The feds didn't just give the money to states to help with preserving education; they insisted the states compete against each other in what was called the Race to the Top (RTTT) competition. The competing states had to agree to major changes in their education policies as a requirement to even apply for the stimulus money.

(ACRONYM ALERT! Bear with me in this next section as I must lay out some key players in the Common Core cult, so I must play their acronym game. Hang in there, put a clothespin on your nose, and put on your knee high boots.)

In their application, the governor of each state had to agree to do the following:

1. **Adopt the not-yet-written Common Core standards.**

   The feds would pay the National Governors Association (NGA) and the CCSSO (Council of Chief State School Officers) to have a group of 29 people, mostly from testing and textbook companies, write the standards in secret. Since these two companies are private, they are not subject to Freedom of Information Act (FOIA) requests so we don't know how they came up with the standards or who was responsible for choosing the group that wrote them. They also own the copyright to the Common Core Standards and states agreed to adopt the standards in total without the ability to amend them. The Common Core technocrats would let states have 15% input into some "state specific" components of the standards, just so long as the Common Core's copyrighted standards comprised 85% of the state standards. Sugar daddy Bill Gates would also chip in money. More on him later.

2. **Band together with other states into testing consortiums where Common Core approved groups would design a test to assess the not-yet-written standards.**

   The two consortiums are called the PARCC (Partnership for Assessment of Readiness for College and Careers) and Smarter Balanced Assessment Consortium (SBAC, or just Smarter Balanced). These two groups are basically identical, just the final versions of their tests will differ slightly. This setup merely gives the appearance that there isn't just one national testing group controlling the assessment of the one set of national standards. That's *too* much centralization *too* soon. The *feds*, through the U.S. Department of Education, paid well over $300 million for the PARCC and Smarter Balanced group to create an assessment, help implement the Common Core Standards, and advocate on behalf of the cult of Common Core. Bill Gates opened his Louis Vuitton man-purse as well.

3. **Set up statewide NSA-like data suctioning systems, the Statewide Longitudinal Data System (SLDS), to suction all manner of information about your children, your family, and your children's teachers into the Common Core machine.**

Longitudinal data systems allow your child, and their personal information, to be tracked from pre-school to college and beyond. The feds chipped in to pay for these systems too. The U.S. Department of Education would change the regulations for the education privacy laws, known as FERPA, so that not only your kids' teachers, but private companies, could tap into your children's private information without your permission or notification. These new data predators may include testing, technology, gaming, research, and assorted computer software companies that enable schools to teach the Common Core standards and take the online Common Core test. This aspect of the cult of Common Core has businesses and politicians alike drooling over the possibility of mining data accumulated on your child from Kindergarten to Career, and beyond. Now does it make sense why Billy Gates is so into education reform these days? Why just settle for being a billionaire when he can be a trillionaire?

4. **Certify that there are no laws barring the linking of student achievement data to teachers and principal evaluations.**

> To ensure that teachers are in compliance with Common Core dictates, states were required to certify that they could legally attach all student achievement to the classroom teacher and the principal in charge of that teacher. Any teacher who "goes rogue" and teaches their kids to think for themselves can be easily identified and corrective action can be taken immediately.

To sweeten the pot, The Department of Education also announced plans to award an additional $5.6 billion in additional grants through several other federal programs to states that fall in line with Obama's plans to fundamentally transform education in our country. Out of this pot of money the federal government would pay for the creation of the two testing consortia (PARCC and Smarter Balanced) to create their national Common Core test and pay for the setup of the national NSA-like student data suctioning systems. In addition, the U.S. Department of Education also gave the conforming states waivers that exempted them from certain conditions of onerous federal education regulations and their penalties, like those in the *No Child Left Behind Act.*

State governors sold off state sovereignty over education to the feds for 30 pieces of silver. They then made the promised changes to their states' education policies using their governor-appointed state boards of education, rather than putting it to the vote in their state legislatures. Why involve the citizenry when they may not make the correct choice for their own children?

Most citizens were too busy dealing with the economic collapse, their lives, and the fight over Obamacare to notice. Besides, the Common Core was still in its theoretical stage. Its standards had not been written yet, its test had not been created, and its data suctioning systems were not fully in place either.

The Common Core standards themselves would not be fully implemented until 2013, and its test would not be given until 2015. That gave the cult of Common Core plenty of time to silently grow their tentacles of control; the reeducation of the public could wait. Many Governors smilingly campaigned their way through the next election cycle bragging about how they saved their states' education departments from the chopping block. I know, because my state's governor, Arizona Governor Jan Brewer-who-eats-scorpions-for-breakfast, did just that.

When anti-Common Core forces began calling for the repeal of the Common Core structures, one of the Common Core groups' main arguments is that there had already been so much money spent on implementing those structures to scrap them now. That's kind of like drugging your wife and paying for her to undergo facial reconstructive surgery as she is sleeping. I know some of you find that appealing, but stick with me on this analogy, please.

When she wakes up and is furious about your fundamental transformation of her face, your reaction is one of incredulity. You shout out, "You don't appreciate what I've done for you? You always talked about getting work done. Now it's been paid for and implemented. You want to throw all that money away and go back to your old face, which really wasn't working for me anyways? You are so ill-informed! You are just some white suburban mom who is discovering her old face wasn't as wonderful as she thought it was! Don't you know your new face is benchmarked to women in Finland? I know that was what you wanted because I data suctioned all of your internet searches!" You kind of get the connection to the Common Core that I'm driving into the ground I hope.

Some states, like Texas, refused to give up their sovereignty over education to the feds. It didn't hurt that their economy was really strong so they could take a pass on the federal money. Choosing not to become part of the cult of Common Core has not seemed to dampen Texas's booming economy and rising population either, just the opposite is true. Alaska, Nebraska, and Virginia's governors also refused to sell off their sovereignty over education, standing firm against federal coercion.

Okay, let's take a deep breath and let all that information sink in. Acronyms will be used sparingly from now on, if at all. Rather than listing every group and person pushing the Common Core, I will mostly refer to them as the Common Core cult, machine, or group, whichever feels best. I will only identify specific people and acronymed groups if it is absolutely necessary to my explanation. Let us forge on. You may now remove the clothespin from your nose, but keep your boots on, we are still in it pretty deep.

4

The Suctioning of Data

"The moment the idea is admitted into society that property is not sacred as the law of God, and that there is not a force of law and public justice to protect it, anarchy and tyranny commence. Property must be secured or liberty cannot exist." John Adams

Each state that applied to receive *Stimulus* money for education agreed to set up NSA-like data suctioning systems, known as Statewide Longitudinal Data Systems, (*SLDS*). These systems would be different from previous state data systems because they would need to be "longitudinal". Visualize a single line of longitude on a map; longitude lines are the vertical lines running north and south. A longitudinal system pulls all of your child's data into a single line or stream of information. You might even visualize a river that is being fed by multiple creeks converging into it, adding to the total volume of the river's flow of water. Longitudinal data systems do the same thing with your child's data, pulling all their various points of data into one stream that is continually added to as they progress from pre-school up through college and career. This system makes tracking all of your child's data easier than the previous system, which had a lot "creeks" of information, but no one single "river" of information to tap into.

In an ideal world, this change would not have been so bad for education because teachers can tap into that stream of data to help inform how they teach your child. If your child's teacher is underperforming, then the data stream will alert their principals to take corrective action. In fact, the cult of Common Core uses these justifications in its demand that these longitudinal systems be put in place.

The sinister side of these longitudinal systems is that the *U.S. Department of Education* broadened its interpretation of the education privacy laws (*FERPA*) in 2011, when it changed its regulations. Many people are confused about the education privacy regulation changes. The educational privacy law, *FERPA,* is a law passed by Congress, protecting the privacy of student data. It can only be changed, or amended, by an act of Congress. The executive branch of government, the president and his cabinet members, is charged with carrying out the laws passed by Congress. The president routinely issues "executive orders" or regulations in which he explains how he will carry out the law. The *U.S. Department of Education*, working on behalf of President Obama, made changes to the regulations describing how they will interpret the education privacy (FERPA) laws. They did not change the *FERPA* law itself, they are not able to.

The *U.S. Department of Education* changed the education privacy regulations in at least two crucial ways. Firstly, it increased the number of players that could have access to your child's centralized personal data to include, not just your child's teachers, but any organization or group tangentially involved in your child's education. This can include testing, technology, textbook, and research companies, just to name a few examples. Secondly, it no longer requires parent notification or permission when it shares your child's personal data with these chosen groups or companies.

U.S. Department of Education Secretary, Arne Duncan explained these regulatory changes in a 2011 letter to states. In it, he says that laws requiring parent permission to share your child's data,

> *"...do not apply to the collection, disclosure, or use of personal information collected from students for the exclusive purpose of developing, evaluating, or providing*

educational products or services for or to students or educational institutions."

These companies can have access to your child's and your personal information which at minimum must include the following 12 points which may be interpreted very broadly:

1. *An unique identifier for every student that does not permit a student to be individually identified (except as permitted by federal and state law);*
2. *The school enrollment history, demographic characteristics, and program participation record of every student;*
3. *Information on when a student enrolls, transfers, drops out, or graduates from a school;*
4. *Students scores on tests required by the Elementary and Secondary Education Act;*
5. *Information on students who are not tested, by grade and subject;*
6. *Students scores on tests measuring whether they're ready for college;*
7. *A way to identify teachers and to match teachers to their students;*
8. *Information from students' transcripts, specifically courses taken and grades earned;*
9. *Data on students' success in college, including whether they enrolled in remedial courses;*
10. *Data on whether K-12 students are prepared to succeed in college;*
11. *A system of auditing data for quality, validity, and reliability;*
12. *The ability to share data from preschool through postsecondary education data systems.*

Parent permission or notification is no longer necessary, so long as the data suctioned from your child is for the purpose of "educational products or services". He then lists some examples of "educational products or services" which may include, but are not exclusive to:

-"Curriculum and instructional materials used by elementary schools and secondary schools"

-"Tests and assessments used by elementary schools and secondary schools to provide cognitive, evaluative, diagnostic, clinical, aptitude, or achievement information about students (or to generate other statistically useful data for the purpose of securing such tests and assessments) and the subsequent analysis and public release of the aggregate data from such tests and assessments"

In their application for federal funding to set up these statewide longitudinal data systems (*SLDS)* the states agreed to funnel all the data gathered in these systems to the Department of Education/Common Core machine and to comply with "all executive orders, regulations, and policies governing these systems". So when the U.S. Department of Education changed its regulations and said that parent permission is no longer required in certain circumstances, the states have already agreed to comply.

Most schools obtain parent notification if their child's photo will be displayed on a school website. These regulatory changes, remarkably, give private companies and others access to your child's most personal data that can include your address, school achievement, cognitive abilities, behavioral issues, and attendance information, all without your permission or notification.

School systems may contract tasks, such as conducting student surveys to get a fuller picture of their feelings and attitudes regarding learning in their school, to outside vendors. Surveys, measuring something as broad as "feelings", might be conducted to gather data on a student's sexual feelings, or their feelings of abandonment due to a parent's divorce, or their feelings about their parents' political leanings on a multitude of topics, such as gun rights. All this data will be added to your child's longitudinal data stream and follow them into college and possibly beyond.

Parents may also unwittingly be adding to their student data flow. When they come in for parent/teacher conferences, they may share personal information about their child that will then be entered into that child's data stream.

In their application for their cut of the $4 billion *Stimulus* money, the states also certified that they could legally attach student achievement and personal data to teachers and the principals who oversee them. This is important because the Common Core needed an enforcement mechanism to alert them when teachers were not complying with their mandates for the classrooms. Not only is student achievement data attached to the teacher, but data regarding instruction in the classroom may be included in addition as grade books and lesson plans are increasingly required to be online.

Schools and states provided aggregated student data routinely to the U.S. Department of Education as part of receiving federal funding for education. Federal funding of state education hovers around 10% for most states. But, previously, states had full control over their stream of information, only sharing that piece of information that was required by federal funding laws. With the new changes in regulations the Common Core machine can now tap into your child's entire stream of data after it flows up to the national level through the longitudinal data suctioning systems. All this would be done without notifying the states that supplied that data to the *feds* and without notifying the parents that supplied that data to the schools and states.

The big shift in data collection is that it is moving directly to the source of the data, your children, to gather personally identifiable information that will be tied to your child and therefore your family. Your child's data file will begin inflating with information starting in universal pre-school, continue filling through to high school, and college with the cult of Common Core tapping into it anytime it wants without your knowledge. Bill Gates is already lobbying to change federal laws so that your child's data can be tracked through college and decades into your career.

Big Testing companies, Pearson and ETS, are already suctioning data on your child if they are taking a Common Core field test this spring. They are using your kids to gather data to improve their tests. That way they can then sell the tests back to the states to use as their official Common Core-aligned test at multi-million dollar profits. Try asking your school or state what the procedure is for you to find out what those private companies are doing with your child's data.

U.S. Senator Ed Markey (D-MA) became so alarmed by reports of the NSA-like data suctioning practices begun the *U.S. Department of Education*, that he addressed a letter to the Secretary of Education, Arne Duncan, asking him to explain the rationale for his changes to the *FERPA* regulations.

We're not done with data yet. It gets worse. The U.S. Department of Education sponsored a study called "Tenacity, Grit, and Perseverance". This study made recommendations on how the Common Core might collect and use "non-cognitive" data.

In this study, the Common Core technocrats envisioned a world in which school kids would "self-report" their feelings about their learning environment with random surveys that may pop up on an assessment or on a digital textbook throughout the day. Students could wear beepers that would go off at random times which would prompt the student to self-report their feelings and maybe record what was causing them to feel frustrated or concerned.

They also foresee possibly using "informant reports" that could be made by someone other than your child like teachers, parents, or other outside observers and added to your child's data file. Is your child withdrawn or anti-social? Let's make an entry into his file.

School records, they contend, can provide important indicators of perseverance over time as well, to include attendance patterns, grades, test scores, social services used, and discipline problems. Wouldn't it be helpful to an establishment political group to release some behavioral records or therapy session notes during your rebellious period in high school should you ever challenge or threaten their positions? Add on to that having access to all of your medical records aggregated under *Obamacare* and the *Internal Revenue Service* (IRS). This would make for a pretty compliant electorate.

In these people's *Brave New World* they envision using neuroscience technology to tap into your child's emotions while they are learning through facial expression technology and mood meters. Does the student look frustrated when they are reading about gun control? Perhaps they can have a "self-report" survey pop up on their computer to ask about their feelings regarding guns or if their parents have guns.

They fantasize about measuring physiological responses to tap into your child's emotions by tracking eye movement, using pressure mouses, posture analysis seats, or using wireless skin conductance sensors that are inside a wristband that your child might wear. There is nothing they cannot know about your child according to these people.

With $100 million, Bill Gates helped start *InBloom*, a company which acts as a middleman between schools and software vendors. They will store student data in the cloud format before funneling it to outside vendors to develop software applications, or other technologies.

At the 2013 SXSW Technology Summit in Texas, Bill Gates interviewed *InBloom*'s CEO during a panel discussion on technology in education. Gates waxed poetic about how all that data that they gathered could be used for research to tap into the estimated $9 billion market that is represented in the K-12 classrooms. All those customers, or rather students, that could benefit from data!

InBloom hopes to become the premiere student data company as it competes state to state for contracts. Unfortunately there have been several instances, most notably in New York, where student personal information has been compromised raising the alarm with data privacy experts at the Electronic Privacy Information Center (EPIC). The CEO of *InBloom* merely shrugs incidences like this off explaining that they never guaranteed student data privacy.

On a public television special, *TED Talks Education*, Bill Gates dreamily described how nice it would be to one day have a camera in every classroom so teachers could tape all their lessons and choose their top lesson to be used in their performance evaluation. I'm sure the other 185 days of taped instruction would be destroyed since it would not be like Big Government to make sure teachers are teaching the appropriate, centrally approved position on man caused global warming would it?

Governor LePage, of Maine, became concerned enough about this trend in data suctioning that he recently signed an executive order forbidding the sharing of personal student data with the feds. His executive order reads in part,

> *"No personally identifiable data on students and/or their families' religion, political party affiliation, psychometric data, biometric information, and/or voting history shall be collected, tracked, housed, reported or shared with the federal government, nor provided to private vendors for the purposes of marketing or business development."*

Big Business, including Big Data, sees the potential to data mine vast amounts of information about students, which is continuously gathered from the classroom and shared with a wide range of outside enterprises. Perhaps Microsoft will be the preferred computer company to provide computer software and hardware in this endeavor, and perhaps have first dibs on all that data.

No wonder major companies are lining up with Bill Gates behind the Common Core and lobbying state legislators to keep it in place. Big Business, through the Chambers of Commerce, has already been attempting to sway increasingly skeptical voters and legislators to back the Common Core with an ad campaign financed with the help of Bill Gates' deep pockets.

Big Government's power would be exponentially increased with the NSA-like suctioning of student data. Imagine having all that academic, behavioral, and self-survey data with which to compile voter profiles on every kid before they even became eligible to vote at 18 years old.

The Department of Education has access to any information that is compiled under the new Common Core data rules. What a treasure trove of voter information, not to mention information on their families, the administration would have access to. Who is to say they can't use InBloom to funnel that information out to one of their educational "non-profits" for future community organizing activities once they are out of office.

David Coleman, Common Core architect and now head of the College Board, bragged about how he used President Obama's *Organizing for America* data gurus to access this data suctioning system to identify low income Hispanic students and pulled them into the social justice arm of the College Board known as *Access to Rigor*. This program is designed to give access to underserved groups, like Hispanics, to bridge the achievement gap, according to Coleman. The *National Hispanic Christian Leadership Conference* then publicly backed the Common Core, go figure.

In his 2015 budget, President Obama wants to increase money to these NSA-like data suctioning tracking systems to continue to "bridge the achievement gap" and also tap into another potential voter block. That way they can tailor their election year talking points to talk directly to those students and their families, crafted by tapping into their data stream. Not to be outdone, Bill Gates is already lobbying to get current laws changed so that his friends at

Big Government can track the data of all college kids during college and decades beyond throughout their careers. Bill Gates and the cult of Common Core are relentless.

5

Pimp Daddy Bill Gates

"Give me control over a nation's currency and I care not who makes its laws." *Baron M. A. Rothschild*

Remember the Bill Gates that we thought we knew growing up? He was the genial, college dropout geek who started a computer software company and brought personal computers into our homes, while becoming a billionaire several times over. In fact, I am using one of his company's computers right now, although I am wearing rubber surgical gloves, and there is a piece of electrical tape over the laptop camera lens.

I have gotten to know a very different Bill Gates as I dug into the cult of Common Core. Now I see him as that creepy old man sitting alone at the edge of the playground with his hands in his pockets asking kids if they want some Common Core candy. He could also be the creepy clown from the movie, *It*, that I mentioned in this book's introduction, coaxing kids and parents alike to come closer to the storm drain opening.

Common Core would not exist if not for Bill Gates' money. In addition to the feds, Bill Gates, an unelected multi-billionaire, has given over $2.3 billion to date to help the Common Core get created, implemented, and favorably advocated for across our country. This is a good investment towards gaining the lion's share of that potential $9 billion student market he salivates over. In 2013 alone he directed $20 million to at least 75 different groups to aid in the implementation of the Common Core. They are listed in Appendix B of this book and their names are a *Who's Who* of the cult of Common Core. How is it permitted for one unelected person to have such influence over our children's education and minds?

The cult of Common Core would have us believe that there were all these educational reform groups, working on a shoestring budget on behalf of the children, until Big Government and Big Business's money decided to help them out. The opposite is true. Big Government and Big Business have complimenting agendas for our children. They teamed up to give billions of dollars to create "non-profits" which could act as front groups to drive their centralized education model providing an endless flow of data suctioned from our children.

The ultimate irony is that Bill Gates dropped out of college so that he could put his originality and his individual talent to work to make his fortune, yet he wants the rest of us to make sure our kids are "college and career ready" by using a one-size-fits-all, homogenized, dumb-downed program that is centrally controlled. In Bill Gates' mind the job of education is to create worker bees and college goers. He said as much when he compared having common education standards for our children to having common standards for things like light switches across the nation. Except that in education our "products that have common standards" are not light switches, they are actual living beings, but why get technical?

Bill Gates sees our kids as products on an assembly line. He wants them produced better and with greater consistency than we have in the past, please. That will make them better consumers of his products, which he will improve using their leeched student data. This doesn't apply Bill Gates own children as they are tucked safely away in an exclusive non-public school in Seattle, free of Common Core mandates.

You see, In Bill Gates' world, there are the ranchers and then there are the cattle. Bill Gates' kids are of the elite rancher class, while your children are cattle steeped in the conformity of Common Core. His kids are being trained make choices for your kids, and your kids are being trained to follow orders. His kids will treat your kids like the products that Bill Gates thinks they are, gaining sustenance from them. If the cattle begin to think for themselves, or to remember their history of individualism and liberty, that would be bad for business and Bill Gates is all about Big Business.

As I mentioned previously, Bill Gates has set his sights on the continuance of data collection/tracking of college kids decades after they leave college and enter into their chosen careers. Bill is following the money. Now Bill Gates isn't just the creepy old man on the playground, he's also hanging outside the student union on our college campuses wearing his all-too-skimpy Dolphin shorts.

One thing I will give to Bill Gates is that he is the most honest high-ranking member in all the cult of Common Core. He is very up front about what he intends to do with student data. At the Conference of State Legislators, Gates said, "For the first time, there will be a large uniform base of customers eager to buy products that can help every kid learn and every teacher get better." We are all customers in Bill's eyes.

Most cultists in Common Core, on the other hand, keep repeating the same talking points while obfuscating their true intentions. While the Common Core machine creates national standards and tests, it wholeheartedly denies that the feds are creating a national curriculum, mainly because it is illegal to do so.

Bill Gates has no such reservations about a national curriculum, explaining,"...identifying common standards is not enough. We'll know we've succeeded when the curriculum and the tests are aligned to these standards. To create just these kinds of tests— next-generation assessments aligned to the common core. When the tests are aligned to the common standards, the curriculum will line up as well."

I could not have said it better myself. Then again, who of you in the cult of Common Core is going to chastise Bill Gates for his lack of adherence to your preprogrammed talking points? He's your Daddy.

6

The Cult's Chicago Connections

"Like corrupt Harlem Congressman Charlie Rangel, who did his best to keep new businesses out of Harlem so that he could fend off rivals and accumulate anti-poverty money for his political friends and allies, liberalism has been dedicated to preserving the problems for which it presents itself as the solution." Fred Siegal, The Revolt Against the Masses

The cult of Common Core has its crude beginnings in Chicago. The central players shaping the cult of Common Core (Bill Coleman, Jason Zimba, US Secretary of Education Arne Duncan, and President Obama) burnished their education reform credentials in Chicago before inflicting this failed model upon the rest of the nation.

President Obama, who never met a current event he didn't like to interject himself into, is publicly mute about the Common Core. Privately he is its key proponent. His administration says he embraces this "new" effort to raise standards for college and career readiness for our children, as if he is an outside party to it. He knows that once he starts advocating for the Common Core it becomes a federal government-pushed initiative, something they have worked hard to disavow.

Once Obama starts advocating for the Common Core there will also be the inevitable comparisons to Obamacare. Both Common Core and Obamacare are federal takeovers, both were written in secret, both had politicians lie about their true intent and consequences, no one can escape either program, and the grassroots opposition is rising up against both programs as the effects of their implementation are felt.

Another initiative that Obama does not talk about, nor does he mention in either of his autobiographies, is his leadership of the Chicago Annenberg Challenge (CAC). From 1995-1999 State Senator Obama was the head of the CAC and remained on its board until 2001.

If President Obama did boast of his leadership role at the Chicago Annenberg Challenge he would also have to acknowledge his close relationship with the unrepentant terrorist, Bill Ayers, in whose house Obama launched his political career. Obama spent his whole 2008 presidential campaign downplaying his relationship with Ayers who he said was just a "guy" in his neighborhood that he never really exchanged ideas with.

Wealthy philanthropist, Walter Annenberg, funded a national education initiative in the mid 1990's to reform education. Bill Ayers, domestic terrorist, founder of the Weather Underground that bombed the Pentagon, was the key force behind attracting Annenberg's millions to Chicago to create the Chicago Annenberg Challenge.

Bill Ayers is one of those 1960's radicals whose actions were completely rejected by American society, who then sunk into academia to rehabilitate his image using education reform as his beard. We still know who you are Bill. And like many of his pony-tailed old has-been compatriots of the sixties, Bill Ayers cannot help but infect everything he touches with his radical, putrid ideology of American oppression while living on his capitalism derived trust fund.

Bill Ayers became the head of the "Collaborative", which directed education policy for the Chicago Annenberg Challenge, and worked in partnership with Barack Obama who, as Chairman of the

Board for the CAC, handled the money. The purported goal of the CAC was to reform education. What Obama and Ayers actually did was channel $100 million to countless groups whose goal was radicalization of education rather than true reformation. Sounding a bit Common Core-ish?

Rather than giving money directly to Chicago's schools, Bill and Barack poured millions of dollars into radical groups like the South Shore African Village Collaborative and Bill Ayers' own Small School Movement that focused less on student academics and more on student activism and victimhood.

In the final analysis, the Chicago Annenberg Challenge was more a failed social justice experiment than an actual education reform success. It ended with "no visible improvement in student performance" according to the CAC itself.

David Coleman and Jason Zimba, both architects of the Common Core, were also in Chicago burnishing their education reform credentials. They negotiated a $2 million agreement with the Chicago Public Schools' CEO, Arne Duncan, to package student data with their new company, *Grow Network*. Arne Duncan would follow President Obama to Washington D.C. to become his Secretary of Education and main Common Core advocate.

Eventually David Coleman and Jason Zimba would sell their *Grow Network* to *McGraw Hill*, a textbook company, before writing the Common Core Standards. After the standards were written, they formed Achievement Partners to push states to implement the Common Core with an $18 million grant from General Electric (GE). Many people who are associated with the Common Core somehow become powerful money magnets.

David Coleman would then go on to head the College Board, which runs the SAT college admission test. Here he is aligning the SAT college admissions test and college admission standards with the Common Core, while simultaneously dumbing the SAT test down to ensure an "expanded opportunity to attend college" for all.

So to make kids "college and career ready" they want to lower the bar to college, not raise the bar of achievement. These Common Core people and their contradictions are like viruses continually mutating and replicating as they spread their infection.

President Obama decided to reconstitute this Chicago team, where no actual student progress was demonstrated, in Washington with him to form the foundation of his education reform machine, the Common Core. They are using similar tactics on a national level as they did in Chicago. They always purport to do one thing like "increase college and career readiness" when their actual agenda is centralized control of education and using it to push their social justice agenda.

Obama has learned that *"he who controls the money, controls the world"*. With the Common Core they have learned to use front groups like the National Governors Association to launder their federal dollars and their will over education into "state-led" initiatives. The Russians are now framing their annexation of Crimea as a "Crimea-led" initiative, so perhaps the Russians are taking a cue in doublespeak from the Common Core crowd. Centrally controlled, authoritative birds of a feather indeed do flock together. Is it pheasant season yet?

7

Deprogramming the Cult's Talking Points

"Satan is never more successful than under the guise of an angel of light. His favorite guise in modern times is that of philanthropy..." Orestes Augustus Brownson, The American Republic

The cult of Common Core has certain talking points that its members robotically recite, *ad nauseam*, when they are posed with questions about their homogenized one-size-fits-all program. Anyone who has had even a casual interaction with one of its cult member knows that familiar feeling of vomit hitting the back of their throat every time they use the word "rigorous" to describe the Common Core. They all seem to be speaking from the same script with their faculty of individual thinking having been anesthetized long ago.

I have gathered many of the Common Core talking points below followed by my rebuttal to each one, based on my own research and personal experience as a teacher. Some of the points in my rebuttals have already been put forth earlier in this book, but are worth repeating for emphasis in this format.

The cult sayeth: The Common Core is a state-led initiative where the states' governors united in the common cause of making our students internationally competitive and college and career ready.

The deprogrammed rebuttal says:

The Common Core was not a "state-led" effort any more than a child cleaning his room in exchange for an allowance and a roof over his head is a "child-led" effort. During the Great Recession, cash strapped states were coerced by the federal government into changing their education policies in exchange for the chance to even apply for $4.3 billion in *Stimulus Act* money in 2009.

Forty-six governors agreed to sell their states' sovereignty over education for 30 pieces of silver. They agreed to adopt the yet-to-written Common Core standards, to become part of a Common Core testing group that would write the test for the yet-to-be-written standards, and they agreed to set up data suctioning systems, State Longitudinal Data Systems (SLDS), to suction all manner of personal student data into the Common Core central command. Standing strong against federal coercion governors of Alaska, Texas, Nebraska, and Virginia refused.

But don't take my word on this, *U.S. Secretary of Education*, Arne Duncan, said as much in a 2010 speech to *UNESCO* (the **U**nited **N**ations **E**ducational, **S**cientific and **C**ultural **O**rganization).

He said,

> "On K-12 education, our theory of action starts with the four assurances incorporated in last year's economic stimulus bill, the American Recovery and Reinvestment Act (2009). The four assurances got their name from the requirement that each governor in the 50 states had to provide an "assurance" they would pursue reforms in four areas-in exchange for their share of funds from a Recovery Act program designed to largely stem job loss among teachers and principals."

To this global body he admitted that the federal government coerced states to change their educational policies in exchange for stimulus money.

He also admitted that these "assurances" had nothing to do with stemming educator job losses, they were coercion. Among the four "assurances" that the *feds* demanded from the states, he listed the requirements to adopt the national standards, to create a national assessment, and to implement data suctioning systems. Arne Duncan always claims that the states were never coerced into changing their education systems in exchange for federal monies. Now we know that Arne Duncan lied.

The cult sayeth: The Common Core standards are more rigorous than all of the states' previous standards.

The deprogrammed rebuttal says:

The Common Core standards are not more rigorous, they are just different. They supposedly only prescribe what is to be learned in k-12 math, reading, and writing. The Thomas Fordham Institute conducted a study in 2010 that compared the Common Core Standards with each of our country's state standards. They found that 13 states' standards were at par or better than the new Common Core standards. They also found that Indiana, California, and the District of Columbia had learning standards that were superior in comparison. Yet these same states' governors dumped their superior standards for Common Core's multi-billion dollar dowry.

Dr. James Milgram, an internationally renowned mathematician who was on the standards validation committee, refused to validate the Common Core standards. He says that under these new standards, our 8th graders will be two years behind the rest of world in math, since taking Algebra1 is no longer a requirement at this grade level, and it only gets worse as they move into the upper grades.

Algebra in eighth grade prepares students to take more advanced classes in high school, which in turn better prepares them for college and possibly a career in science, technology, engineering or math. At the end of high school our kids, under the Common Core, will not be prepared to pursue math, science, or technology careers, or be prepared to apply to highly selective colleges which require a background in high level math such as Calculus.

But let's listen to Common Core architect, Jason Zimba himself, echoing this criticism that, "If you're a young person who wants to become an engineer, or who wants admission to an elite university, you would be advised to take mathematics beyond the (Common Core requirement) level...you will need to take more mathematics than is in the Common Core."

Since Common Core doesn't require an Algebra1 course until high school, unlike most advanced countries and many state standards before Common Core, our kids are at a disadvantage. Common Core just isn't rigorous enough for college and career readiness. There, not only did I get in the weeds regarding standards, I used the cult of Common Core's jargon to do it. How's your math anxiety? Mine is high right now, but hold on, only a bit more to go.

The cult of Common Core once salivated (they do this a lot) over getting Dr. Milgram's endorsement, but now that he opposes the standards they take every opportunity to impugn his reputation. Cults do not like when former insiders betray them and will use any means necessary to smear and intimidate them into silence. I know this from experience, but more on that later.

The Common Core group confuses "more rigorous" with "more complicated". In math they boast about how their standards teach less math concepts at each grade level than before, but they teach them deeper. A kid can't just know that 12-9=3, they have to demonstrate their knowledge of this concept by showing it 5 different ways visually. Many of these ridiculous math problems are posted daily online for the world to see by bewildered parents of equally bewildered children.

Arguing about the nuances of each standard is a favored technique of the Common Core crowd when confronted by the opposition. Two people can have different interpretations of any learning standard. As long as the discussion is focused on the minutia of each standard, the Common Core group does not have to talk about how the standards have never been tested anywhere in the world before and proven to improve student learning.

They cannot talk about testing the standards because the common core standards were just recently written, and the tests designed to asses them have not been finalized yet. They are asking for us to just trust them when they claim that their standards are more rigorous than, and an improvement upon the states' previous standards. At least the previous standards had a track record of performance.

A learning standard is not rigorous on its own. A learning standard merely states what a student must know at a minimum at each grade level, as in "the student must be able to recall the product of two single digit factors from memory (for example, 3X4=12)". The teacher can then make the learning more rigorous by having the student extend their understanding by applying the knowledge to the real world. The Common Core group erroneously credits every example of good teaching as an example of the Common Core's more rigorous standards.

The math standards are obviously not written by classroom teachers, as they require a Common Core translation manual and all too many professional development classes to still not come close to understanding them.

Here is what a fifth grade Common Core math standard says a ten-year-old should be able to do in Geometry, provided that the adult teacher knows what the standard means:

The student shall be able to...*"Recognize volume as additive. Find volumes of solid figures composed of two non-overlapping right rectangular prisms by adding the volumes of the non-overlapping parts, applying this technique to solve real world problem."*

Quick, begin teaching it right now....and go! The only thing more rigorous in Common Core math is the use of a thesaurus by some pompous, Common Core standard writer. Any wonder teachers have no idea what to teach in their classrooms? Any wonder that districts are paying big bucks to buy Common Core "aligned" textbooks and software programs to try and go for the quick fix? There's no wonder why textbook and online learning companies are shilling for Common Core. They are filling this confusion void with their products and filling their bank accounts in the process.

The Common Core says it is only concerned with the learning standards that deal with reading, writing, and math. They say that they have no ambition to also write standards and control what kids learn in the politically charged areas of social studies and science. But these are the exact areas that they really want to control.

Common Core requires an increasing focus on informational reading and writing, so that it comprises 50% of all reading and writing in the elementary grades and increases up to 70% by the twelfth grade. Therefore, the Common Core group demands that, starting in sixth grade, students' writing be infused with social studies and science content. This is a backdoor way of controlling what the kids will learn in these two fields. I can imagine a centrally controlled Common Core machine "infusing" kids' readings with political content that is in line with the President's position on green energy, immigration, or healthcare.

The cult sayeth: The Common Core does not create a national curriculum.

The deprogrammed rebuttal says:

The "standards" refer to what kids should know and the "curriculum" refers to how they obtain that knowledge or skill, or rather how they are taught. It is illegal for the government to set a national curriculum according to the 1965 Elementary and Secondary Education Act (ESEA). This is the reason the Common Core continuously mouths this talking point.

The fact of the matter is that the feds have funded the creation of the national Common Core standards and the creation of the tests that assess those standards. The feds have also paid for teacher leadership cadres to develop unit plans, lesson plans, and reading lists aligned to the Common Core as exemplars for other teachers to emulate in the classroom. Many of these are the sources of the ridiculous Common Core lessons and math problems we have been seeing shared on social media. If this isn't federal government involvement in the curriculum, what is?

Any teacher will tell you that the curriculum and the standards are intertwined and are not easily separated. So if the federally funded Common Core group controls the standards, which come before the teaching, and they control the test, which comes after the teaching, then they will control the teaching, which is the curriculum.

Most teachers are still waiting for the Common Core test to come out so that they can tailor their teaching to match the skills kids will need to do well on the test. The test scores will play a big part in how well teachers will rate on their teacher evaluations and the test scores will also be tied to teacher pay.

Bill Gates has stated that the goal is for classroom instruction to align to the test. I have also heard this in my interactions with the Common Core technocrats while working on the Common Core/PARCC test. My Common Core handlers continuously told me that they expect teachers to adjust their instruction to match the style and content of the test. The test and the standards were not designed to reflect what was being taught in the classroom from the bottom up, but rather they were the hammer that shaped the instruction in the classroom from the top down.

The cult sayeth: The Common Core standards were written with input from teachers and other education stakeholders.

The deprogrammed rebuttal says:

The Common Core standards were written in secret, starting in July 2009, and we don't know a thing about their deliberations since the National Governors Association (NGA) is a private group and is not subject to freedom of information requests. The authors of the standards were the 29 member Standards Development Work Group. This group consisted of 14 reps from testing companies (the SAT, ACT, College Board), 10 reps from Common Core groups (Achieve Inc., Student Achievement Partners), 2 reps from a textbook company (America's Choice), 2 reps were educational consultants, and 1 rep was a professor (UC Davis). (See the list of Common Core standards authors in Appendix A.)

Of the 29 people writing the standards, only one was an actual teacher from a university, and not a single K-12 educator with teaching experience was on the committee. There was an advisory group, which gave feedback on the standards, but final decisions regarding the common core standards document was made by the 29-member Standards Development Work Group.

Some states may have accepted feedback at their Departments of Education, back in 2009/2010, during the eight or so months between the announcement of the Common Core Standards Writing Group and the final product delivered in March, 2010. The state departments of education may have even asked for feedback in the couple months following the creation of the standards and the quick adoption of them by their state boards of education. There are some advertisements running where teachers brag about giving such feedback. But the fact worth repeating is that the 29 member Standards Writing Group, which did not have a single K-12 teacher on it, had final say on the standards and could decide to consider or not consider any and all feedback that was presented to them. That's not me talking; that is according to the National Governors Association's (NGA) own press release in July of 2009.

Back in the summer of 2010, I was at the Arizona Department of Education working on our state standardized test (AIMS), as part of a teacher test-creation group, when I heard that our state adopted these "new" standards. We had no idea what the standards entailed, many teachers still don't. How could we give informed, intelligent feedback?

Many of the AZ Department of Education assessment workers that I interacted with were not moved by the adoption of the Common Core standards. The 2012 elections were coming up and the whole centralized Common Core education delivery system may be a moot point if President Obama and his Chicago team were given their walking papers. There was a "wait and see" approach to the new standards. Besides, we were still expected to teach our previous state standards and we were working on the state test that would assess those standards. The Common Core would be rolled out over the next three years, so we could cross that bridge later.

I had an insider's view of our department of education during this time. If I couldn't form an intelligible commentary about the new Common Core standards, how could an teacher or parent on the our outside? Besides, this all occurred during the battle over Obamacare and the meltdown of our economy. We had a lot going on in the country.

There should have been a lot more debate over something as important as dumping all of our state standards for a set of new, untried set of standards written in secret. When Massachusetts overhauled its standards over a decade ago, they debated and collected feedback for over two years. But as I look back, I'm realizing that it was all a calculated strategy by the Obama administration.

The deadline to apply for billions of dollars in federal money was in January 2010, three months before the standards were even created. The states had to agree to adopt the Common Core standards in their applications for their share of the $4 billion *Stimulus* funds. The feds were due to announce which states were to receive federal money in the summer of 2010. Those states that quickly adopted the Common Core Standards before the summer had a distinct advantage over those that waffled. So there was a mad rush by state governors to shove the Common Core standards through to adoption.

It was total coercion by the Obama administration designed to restrict genuine feedback and possible opposition. It was also better for our governors to quickly adopt the standards, get the *fed's* money, and deal with the political fallout later should it come. The governors could always campaign, in 2012, on the fact that they "saved" teacher jobs with the feds money. Many governors, like mine, did just that.

So now, as parents and teachers are more informed about the Common Core, they are rising up in opposition. A common strategy of the cult of Common Core is to contend that feedback was taken back in 2010 when the standards were developed, so no one should complain now. Since when is there a statute of limitations on having an opinion about the takeover of our children's education?

The cult sayeth: The Common Core learning standards are research based and are internationally benchmarked.

The deprogrammed rebuttal says:

The Common Core learning standards are not research based. The Common Core standards were finalized in June 2010 and the assessment that will test the standards impact on student learning is still being written at the time of this book's publication.

These standards have never been implemented, tested, and shown to improve student learning any place in the world. There is no data supporting the efficacy of these standards. The Common Core group scrapped their member state's previous standards, which had a long record of implementation, testing, and measurement of student growth, for a new group of standards which have never been proven to help students learn better. They are asking our kids to test pilot these new standards.

States across the country are pimping out our kids to *Pearson and ETS* to field test the testing companies' unadopted Common Core assessments, the PARCC and Smarter Balanced tests. The testing companies will then use data derived from these field tests to tweak their PARCC and Smarter Balanced tests. They will then turn around and sell the finalized version of those tests back to the states at great profit.

No data from the piloted tests, regarding academic knowledge or computer skills, will be shared with the participating schools. No reimbursement will be given to the schools for their students' participation. Who knows what other data Pearson will be suctioning from our kids?

One of the requirements of being a "governing member" of the Common Core testing groups is that states agree to pilot and then implement the Common Core tests that they create. Don't we have enough problems in education without adding exposing our children to predatory testing companies to that list?

The Common Core group also touts the standards as being internationally benchmarked, as if that is a good thing, without offering the name of a single nation they are benchmarked to. Progressives have a fixation with everything international. The term "internationally benchmarked" just means that the Common Core standards are comparable on paper with other nameless countries' learning standards and that we aspire to their results in education. If we want to emulate Finland, for example, we would emulate, or benchmark, to their standards. Finland seems to be a country the cult of Common Core mentions a lot. How about we all pitch in for a one-way ticket to Finland to all of them?

I could make the case before the U.S. Olympic selection committee that I am internationally benchmarked to a Russian gold medalist figure skater on paper. I could provide evidence that my "rigorous" workout, diet, and practice regimen is identical to the Russian gold medal winner. I could print up copies of his skating routines that he used to win the gold medal along with the music he used and make them my own, on paper.

I could then go before the U.S. Olympic committee and demand a place on the United States figure skating team based on my international benchmarking of the Russian gold medalist. After they finished laughing, the Olympic committee would probably ask where my skating ability had ever been tested and shown to be of gold medal quality. They would ask for data. If I asked that they just take a chance on me to see how I perform, there would be another round of laughter before security was called.

As ridiculous as this scenario sounds, this is exactly what the cult Common Core is asking us to do with our children's education, just trust them. They want us to take their word that these standards are "more rigorous" and will be better for our kids than the previous state standards because they are internationally benchmarked. Only we are not talking about a place on a skating team, we are talking about our children's minds and our country's exceptionalism!

The cult sayeth: The Common Core standards and tests are flexible. States can tailor them to the needs of their states.

The deprogrammed rebuttal says:

Everyone opposing the Common Core should print out a copy of the Common Core' own report, *Coming Together to Raise Achievement*, written by the *K-12 Center* at *ETS* (Education Testing Services). It is in the "Notes" section at the end of this book. Pat Forgione is the Executive Director of the K-12 Center and his wife is Kathy Forgione, one of the authors of the Common Core standards. They keep it all in the family at the cult of Common Core.

This report details the cult's version of the history of the Common Core standards development and details what states gain and what they give up in the way of sovereignty with regards to the standards and the national test that will assess them. This is a great document to cite from when confronting the cult of Common Core.

In the section titled *"What Do States Gain and Give Up?"* this report says,

> *"As required by the CCSSI (Common Core), these states agreed to adopt the complete set of the CCSS (Common Core standards) in ELA and mathematics and may augment them with state-specific standards, provided that the CCSS (Common Core standards) comprise at least 85% of the total."*

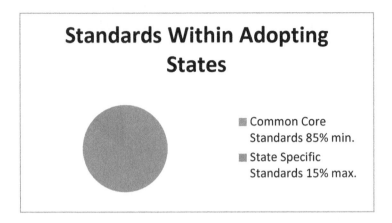

Standards Within Adopting States

■ Common Core Standards 85% min.

■ State Specific Standards 15% max.

So just to be clear, 85% of your state standards are owned by the Common Core. The Common Core owns the copyright and you cannot change a word. The Common Core will let you have input on 15% of your state standards. You don't even have full control over the 15% state-specific standards, as those standards are also mandated to be rooted in the Common Core standards. When is having 15% input into state standards better than having 100% input and control? Only in Common Core math, I guess.

Your state used to have 100% control over its state test, now you are one of 20 (or more) states that have input on your test. When is being one out of twenty better than being the only one having 100% input in creating your state test? Only in Common Core math.

The Common Core continually repeats that their test will cost about the same as the states' previous tests. They don't mention all the other costs that must be shouldered by the states. This report details those further burdens placed on the states,

> *"One significant cost for some states will be the increased level of technology infrastructure required to support these online assessment and reporting systems...(federal) funds will pay for the design, development, and piloting of the assessment systems and related tools and supports, but the*

*subsequent implementation costs are assumed by the
member states."*

Another financial burden that will be passed onto the states will
be scoring the Common Core test. There will be much more in the
way of essay-type responses required of our kids on these tests.
These responses must be scored by actual humans, costing more
money in the way of training and salaries, adding to the test's final
price tag. Ask your state pro-Common Core state official to show
you the cost analysis of the total price tag for implementation and
continual running of the Common Core jalopy they bought for your
state. I can guarantee they don't have one that includes the
complete cost.

States will now shoulder the burden of creating a technology
infrastructure to administer and score a computerized test. States
will also lose control of 85% of their learning standards. In what
universe does this add up to states having flexibility with their
standards and tests? It does in the alternate universe of Common
Core.

The cult sayeth: Data collection will enable teachers to access data
about their students to make teaching decisions and have quick
information about students who move across state lines.

The deprogrammed rebuttal says:

I agree in part with the purported reason for setting up
longitudinal data systems. But personal student data should only be
shared with educators who are directly involved with the education
of your child, sharing it with anyone else should always require your
notification and approval. Using aggregate, anonymous data to
share with state policy makers is also a good idea so they can steer
education in the correct direction. There needs to be strict controls
over the information shared at the federal level and they should

never be given access to your child's stream of personal data unless the parents give direct permission.

But, like with most things Common Core, there is the stated reason and then there's the reality. Your child's data is your property, not the school's, and not to the cult of Common Core. Only a very small percentage of students move across state lines, generally they move within the state. If it takes a couple of extra days to get a student's information from another state, it is well worth what the states maintain in the way of sovereignty and control over personal student data.

The Common Core group has shown that their true intentions with regard to data are less than honorable. The Common Core has changed the education privacy (FERPA) regulations in 2011, so that student data can be shared with private companies and other outside groups who are only tangentially involved with your child's education, all without parent permission. They have also expanded the type of information they can gather about your children that has the potential to be invasive to their privacy and the privacy of your family.

The real goal of expanded data collection by the Common Core machine is to suction information about your child and your family for use by Big Government, which already has an abysmal record for politicizing personal information to quiet its opposition. Big Business wants your child's information purely for financial gain and they will parrot any Big Government talking point they are given if it helps their bottom line.

The cult sayeth: U.S. students are lagging behind the rest of the world in test scores and in the awareness that they are international/global citizens.

The deprogrammed rebuttal says:

This is a favorite whine of progressives in general, and the Common Core group in particular. The test they always cite is the Program for *International Student Assessment*, or the *PISA* test. It is a Eurocentric test in math, science, and writing, given every three years to randomly selected 15-16 year olds from sixty-five participating countries. Countries like Finland, Singapore, and South Korea are always cited as doing so much better than the U.S. on these tests. The Common Core crowd then surmises that we should, therefore, mimic these countries' education policies so that we can measure up.

Like any test, or poll for that matter, the numbers can be interpreted to reflect the desired outcome you would like to see. If the *PISA* results are broken down by ethnicity, for instance, our Hispanic kids' scores beat every other predominantly Hispanic country in the world. Our Asian kids' scores beat every predominantly Asian country except for the students in Shanghai, China. Our Caucasian kids' scores beat every predominantly Caucasian country in the world except for students in Finland. Damn Finland! We could even dissect Finland's advantage. It is a small, homogenized country with a 99% Caucasian population and some of the most restrictive immigration laws in the world. Why not compare our top 1,000 kids to their top 1,000 kids?

At the end of the day I say let Finland, South Korea, and others lead the world in test taking. The American school system, though not perfect, has always produced the innovators, the creators, and those who think outside the box. The American school system created the kids, who became the adults, who created the laptops, which channel the internet we created, that those champion test-taking countries use to take their tests.

Americans aren't lagging behind the rest of the world in international awareness either, we are simply aware that we live in an exceptional country, unlike any country before in the history of the world. This attitude drives American progressives and the rest of the world crazy. You progressives can take another dose of government approved-and-paid-for anti-depressants, because it's the truth. More on this global citizen mindset in the next chapter.

The cult sayeth: A common set of national standards is the hallmark of top performing countries. The Common Core is a vast improvement over the 50 individual states, and their multitude of educational environments, that existed previously in our country.

The deprogrammed rebuttal says:

America's greatness lies in what we *do* in the world, not in our learning standards written on paper. The diversity of our "educational environments" that the Common Core group seems to find is our weakness as a nation, is actually our greatest strength.

Americans like to have their own points of view on every topic under the sun. We argue, debate, advocate for ourselves loudly and proudly. It's not always organized, orderly, or pretty, but that is America.

America is the most racially and religiously diverse nations in the world. The decentralized nature of our state education systems better respects our diversity and breeds originality and individualism, the exact opposite of the centralized, one-size-fits-all, homogenized national Common Core model. Homogenized, orderly nations don't save the world from tyrants; they breed tyrants that America has to save the world from.

The hallmark of a top country is not having good test takers, but rather "doing things" like putting a man on the moon, creating the internet, Google, Apple, and the world's top military and economy. That's what we "do" as Americans and the rest of the world should be copying us, not the other way around.

The cult sayeth: The vast majority of teachers support the Common Core.

The deprogrammed rebuttal says:

   Teachers fear retribution should they speak out against their secretary of education or governor, who are our boss's, boss's boss, and who are in support of the Common Core. They also fear responding honestly to polls sent to them, via their school email, from their department of education. So any polling data citing teachers support for the Common Core presented by state officials should be viewed with suspicion.

   I wrote a commentary opposing the Common Core in a state newspaper here in Arizona. Within days I received a phone call from Sarah Gardner, Arizona Director of PARCC Assessments at the AZ Department of Education, in my classroom regarding my commentary. I was asked to explain my problems with the Common Core. In a robotic, interrogation-style tone, I was asked if I was implementing and teaching the standards in my classroom. I was asked to explain my knowledge of the standards. I found these questions baffling because Sarah Gardner was the same person who sent me to Chicago to work on the Common Core/PARCC test just months earlier on behalf of the Department of Ed. Of course I understand the Common Core standards, Sarah. You sent me to Chicago, not once, but twice, for a week each time to represent our state on the PARCC test review committee. This conversation took place in my classroom as my class was waiting outside the door wanting to come back in from recess.

   This was a blatant attempt at intimidation. When I confronted our state Superintendent of Instruction, John Huppenthal, at a public meeting outside Tucson, he pretended not to know the person who contacted me. Sarah Gardner is his chief director of the PARCC test for the entire state. What other high level state employees does our Huppenthal not know? I don't have direct proof yet, but I believe that Huppenthal may have encouraged the phone call to me. State bureaucrats don't call teachers in their classroom on their own volition. I emailed our Huppenthal the next day to formally protest the attempt at intimidation by his employee. I have yet to get a response from Mr. Huppenthal, but he is up for re-election this year. Perhaps I'll file my complaint at the ballot box on Election Day.

The cult sayeth: Teachers of the Year are in support of the Common Core across the country.

The deprogrammed rebuttal says:

Throw up just hit the back of my throat, but I'll carry on. The cult of Common Core is using its cadre of "Stepford teachers", from the Teachers of the Year program, to spread out across the country to counter growing opposition to the Common Core. They profess to represent teachers and the teaching profession. One Common Core group, Achieve, Inc., lists quotes from these Teachers of the Year who support their standards on their website and claims that "National and state Teachers of the Year represent the most exemplary teaching occurring in classrooms."

The Teacher of the Year program is a project of the Council of Chief State School Officers (CCSSO), which authored the Common Core Standards and holds their copyright. In the interest of full disclosure shouldn't these Teachers of the Year, who are writing Op EDs and lobbying legislatures across the country in support of the Common Core, disclose their connection to the Common Core?

Teachers of the Year applicants must complete a written application, write essays, and jump through political hoops in front of interview committees in order to be considered for their shiny titles and thousands of dollars in gifts and prizes, just like the governors did when they sold out their states in exchange for "prizes" and money in adopting the Common Core. So the Teachers of the Year are perfect shills to recruit for and lobby on behalf of the cult of Common Core. Does anyone seriously believe that the Teacher of the Year organization would choose someone who was against the Common Core?

The Teachers of the Year are supposedly advocates for all teachers and the entire teaching profession. Not all teachers support the Common Core, yet the Teachers of the Year never offer a voice to those who oppose the Common Core machine. Most teachers around the country are humbly and quietly living "teachers of the year" every day in their classrooms. They don't have the time or egos to chase a shiny title.

The cult sayeth: Teacher unions support the Common Core.

The deprogrammed rebuttal says:

Teacher unions do not look out for the best interests of our children, they look out for the interests of their member teachers. If unions feel it will benefit their power by way of access to the political class and monetary favors, they will support the Common Core. They rarely speak to what is best for our children in the classroom, unless it is being used to advocate for what is best for their teachers.

Some teacher unions, like New York's state public teachers union, are starting to formally oppose the Common Core. They oppose the requirement that teacher evaluations and pay are now to be connected to student test scores, so their opposition is tenuous at best. Let's not forget that unions also opposed Obamacare until they got special exemptions from it.

The cult sayeth: The Chamber of Commerce and Big Business supports the Common Core.

The deprogrammed rebuttal says:

The Chamber of Commerce is not looking out for the best interest of our children. They look out for the bottom lines of their member companies. The Chamber of Commerce is a private group that lobbies federal and state representatives to push for the bottom line of their member businesses, as any good capitalist group would. The more they tow Big Government's line on the Common Core, the more legislative access and favors will flow their way.

Big Business stands to rake in billions with the Common Core centralization of education. Big Data and Big Technology, with the likes of Bill Gates, have already identified an untapped $9 billion market in K-12 education.

Big Textbook, companies like McGraw Hill and Carnegie textbooks, is drooling over the possibility of only having to deal with one entity, the Common Core group, when designing and selling their Common Core aligned textbooks. They used to have to deal with 50 states and sometimes hundreds of more school districts. Why wouldn't they suck up to the Common Core now? It's just smart business.

Big Testing, companies like Pearson and Educational Testing Services (ETS), will reap countless more millions as they already have the monopoly over creating and administering the national tests produced by the Common Core test creating groups, PARCC and Smarter Balanced. When I worked on the PARCC test, ETS and Pearson were the only testing companies running the show.

Big Business and Big Government are colluding through Common Core to take over education, just as Big Insurance colluded with Big Government through Obamacare to take over healthcare. They are being helped by progressive elected officials in both the Republican and Democratic parties who are beginning to feel the pushback from the anti-Common Core forces. Former Florida governor and 2016 presidential aspirant, Jeb Bush, for example, has his *Foundation for Excellence in Education* filling the airwaves with pro-Common Core ads.

Bill Gates has already given $1.3 million dollars to the US Chamber of commerce to push the Common Core talking points and has given a total of nearly $2.3 billion to date to thousands of organizations to push the Common Core. You may have already seen ads developed with this money. Big Government has given over $300 million to the PARCC and Smarter Balanced testing groups to not only develop the Common Core test, but to promote the Common Core nationally.

Isn't it ironic that Big Business supports the Common Core standards ostensibly because they create a more educated, "college and career ready" workforce while simultaneously supporting Amnesty for illegal immigrants who come to the country with very little or no education or college and career readiness? The truth is that Big Business is raking in billions from both ends of the spectrum. From the bottom end they get cheap workers and from the top end they get reap billions with Big Data, Big Technology, Big Testing, and Big Textbook.

The cult sayeth: The opposition to the Common Core is a small but vocal minority.

The deprogrammed rebuttal says:

Opposition to the cult of Common Core is vocal, but certainly not a minority. The leaders of the opposition are the moms. Some call them the Mama Grizzlies; I lovingly call them the Badass Mothers. Moms are the ones for the most part who help with homework and volunteer in their children's classrooms, and were the first to sense that something was very wrong in their children's schools. Teachers were still grappling with the imposition of the Common Core themselves so they couldn't really articulate their discomfort. Plus, most teachers are not accustomed to defying their districts, secretaries of education, or their governors.

It was okay to vocally support the Common Core, but should you dare speak in opposition to them, you risked retribution at contract renewal time. Slowly teachers began talking to parents in private and the moms became mouthpieces for the teachers who were too afraid to speak out. When the moms began speaking, out they were maligned by U.S. Secretary of Education, Arne Duncan, as a bunch of "white suburban moms" who are finding out that their children and their schools aren't as brilliant as they thought they were. I wonder what he called the moms in Chicago who didn't think the Chicago Public Schools, which Duncan headed, measured up.

The Common Core crowd, in their arrogance, became accustomed to not being challenged as they grabbed control of our children's education. The rest of us were busy living our lives and trusted that those we elected to office as governors and secretaries of education were looking out for our kids. The truth of the matter is that, just like with Obamacare, our leaders were lazy, uninformed, easily coerced, and often times dishonest. Rather than admit their mistakes, many have doubled down on stupid and stand steadfast in their support of the Common Core.

Governors adopted the Common Core and let the cult through the gates by using their state boards of education without a single vote in their state legislatures. Currently, 10 state legislatures have dropped the Common Core test and 33 states have legislation pending to either pause or end the Common Core standards or test. Texas, Alaska, Virginia, and Nebraska refused to sell their sovereignty over education and their states' economies and their students' learning has not suffered, in fact they have outpaced the Common Core member states.

Opposition to the Common Core is grassroots. You won't hear much about this opposition in the Big Government controlled media. You will hear about it online with alternative and social media. Michelle Malkin, Glenn Beck's *The Blaze*, and *Breitbart* News have been leading the charge against the Common Core, armed with the facts.

Truth in American Education has an excellent aggregating website listing many anti-Common Core groups, news, and legislation occurring nationally. They should be on your favorites list. Every state has a multitude of groups coalescing to stop the Common Core, usually started by moms. There are numerous blog sites and state groups opposing the Common Core only a Google search away.

Respected education experts like Dr. Sandra Stotsky and Dr. James Milgram are crisscrossing the country sounding the alarm against the Common Core and taking the slings and arrows too. There is also a growing national opt-out of testing movement catching fire.

Indiana Governor Mike Pence just recently signed legislation removing his state from the Common Core standards and test. Eight U.S. senators, including Ted Cruz and Rand Paul, have signed onto Sen. Chuck Grassley's (R-Iowa) fight to defund the Common Core. Senator Ed Markey (D-MA) is challenging the U.S. Department of Education over data suctioning.

Rep. Jeff Duncan (R-S.C.) introduced a resolution, with 43 other Congressmen signing on, denouncing how the U.S. Department of Education coerced states into adopting the Common Core in exchange for federal monies.

In every state there are brave state legislators who are challenging their governors with legislation to disentangle their states' children from the cult of Common Core. They need your support and voices.

8

The World Board of Education

"The first time someone shows you who they are, believe them." Maya
Angelou

The cult of Common Core is an internationally focused bunch.
They are always looking to the rest of the world for models in
education or environmental stewardship as benchmarks for
America. America rarely measures up to these people. In fact,
according to them, we are the source of most problems in the
world, consuming more than our fair share of resources and
expelling more than our fair share of pollutants, causing the climate
to change overnight. I wonder if they know that a passport will get
them out of this "horrible" country so that they can go to their
nirvana somewhere in the middle of Finland, no doubt.

The Common Core crowd, with their slight-America-first
mentality, feels that our kids fall short in their international
awareness and in their roles as global citizens. This is their way of
saying that America needs to get over itself, we are not exceptional,
and we should demonstrate our place in the world, as just another
country, by falling in line with the 'global' view on everything from
man-caused global warming to living in a 'sustainable' or 'green'
way."

The terms "sustainability" and "green" are used a lot by home-grown and world progressives alike. To them, sustainability means that advanced countries and their people should alter everything about the way they live in "fairness" to poorer countries and in order to sustain the environments and cultures of the world for future generations. Of course there are centralized global groups that will be just the people to tell us how we should live, what is fair, how we should leave the world for future generations, and who should be born into those future generations. It's a centrally controlled, world view where national boundaries are obsolete.

Just as the American cult of Common Core has the twin goals of national homogenization and conformity, so too does the global cult of Common Core have similar goals of international conformity and homogenization. Only they are much closer to their goals and are just waiting for their little sister Common Core in the United States to come around and join up with the global family.

The global version of the cult of Common Core is *UNESCO* (the *U.N.'s Education, Scientific, and Cultural Organization*). The sustainability movement appointed *UNESCO as* its task master for world *Sustainability Education,* and has as its central role the implementation of a worldwide plan called, *Agenda 21.*

What is Agenda 21? In short, back in 1992, the *U.N.* sponsored a summit on man-caused global warming in Rio De Janeiro, Brazil. Countries, environmentalists, and other far-left progressive groups from around the world sent representatives. The summit concluded that countries of the world needed to change their self-centered ways to combat man-caused climate change. Countries of the world, they proclaimed, should live in more "sustainable" ways to help preserve the world for future generations.

The summit leaders then revealed the document, called Agenda 21 (as in agenda for the 21st century), which contained all the action steps for implementation and monitoring systems necessary for compliance, that could be installed in their home countries at the local, state, and national levels. Remember that progressivism does not acknowledge national borders, it's a worldwide agenda.

The problem is that sustainability is an intentionally broad concept and can apply to pretty much every area of life from the food that we produce and eat, to the resources we use, to our standards of living, to how many kids we have, and to how we treat each other. It's basically a desire for centrally controlled, homogenization, and conformity dressed up as a concern for Mother Earth's children and taking on names such as "green", "sustainability", "education for all", and "global citizenry".

Agenda 21 is a voluntary action plan, yet many communities around the world have started implementing it under the guise of saving the world through sustainability and "going green". The idea is to quietly advocate at the various levels of government to change regulations and laws to reflect this global agenda of control. Progressives in power may give monetary rewards to those who fall in line. Perhaps citizens will get a tax credit for buying an electrical car, companies will get tax breaks and public praise for "going green", and even schools will get "Green Ribbon" awards for sustainability/environmental education and making their schools "green". Sound familiar?

Since the world's citizens needed to be "re-educated" regarding UNESCO's definition of sustainability, transforming the world's mindset by transforming education would be central before the implementation of *Agenda 21's* plan could be successful. As *UNESCO proclaims,* "There are over 60 million teachers in the world and every one is a key agent for bringing about the changes in lifestyles and systems we need. For this reason, innovative teacher education is an important part of educating for a sustainable future."

UNESCO became the world's centralized, re-education body for Agenda 21. That is why I call UNESCO the *World Board of Education.*

President Reagan thought that *UNESCO* was corrupt and anti-American, so he withdrew our country from it in the early 1980's. President George W. Bush re-enlisted our country into *UNESCO* in 2004, and our membership has held firm through the Obama administration. Both Bush and Obama have overseen the biggest federal intrusion into education since 1965. Progressives are in both the Republican and Democratic Parties; don't be fooled by the jersey they wear on Election Day.

U.S. Secretary of Education, Arne Duncan, seems to be fully in line with the World Board of Education's sustainability plan. He gave a speech to them in 2010 using all the catch phrases. Arne Duncan said:

> *"Today, education is a global public good unconstrained by national boundaries...There is so much that the United States has to learn from nations with high-performing education systems...American students are lagging behind in the implementation of 'sustainable development education'...Countries like Singapore and Finland are leading the way...The United States cannot, acting by itself, dramatically reduce poverty and disease or develop sustainable sources of energy. America alone cannot combat terrorism or curb climate change. To succeed, we must collaborate with other countries...These new partnerships must also inspire students to take a bigger and deeper view of their civic obligations-not only to their countries of origin but to the betterment of the global community."*

Then Arne Duncan starts to sound very Common Core-like when he suggests that,

> *"Those new partnerships require American students to develop better critical thinking abilities, cross-cultural understanding, and facility in multiple languages. They also will require U.S. students to strengthen their skills in science, technology, engineering, and math—the STEM fields "*

But wait a minute. I thought our students were developing their skills in critical thinking and science/technology in order to be college ready or to be a part of a more educated workforce that will make our country internationally competitive. What's all this stuff about becoming better global citizens, who consider their civic obligations to their "country of origin" as being just as important as their obligations to the "global community"? That doesn't sound very internationally competitive to me, rather its sounds quite global.

That was Arne Duncan talking to the world; now let's see what he said here at home, in Washington, D.C., to a Sustainability Summit in 2010. U.S. Secretary of Education, Arne Duncan said:

> *"...we recognize the importance education plays in the sustainability movement. Until now, we've been mostly absent from the movement to educate our children to be stewards of our environment and prepare them to participate in a sustainable economy. Educators have a central role in this. They teach students about how the climate is changing. They explain the science behind climate change and how we can change our daily practices to help save the planet...We at the Education Department are energized about joining these leaders in their commitment to preparing today's students to participate in the green economy, and to be well-educated about the science of sustainability. We must advance the sustainability movement through education."*

If I didn't know any better, I would think that our U.S. Secretary of Education was acting as the mouthpiece of the World Board of Education. Or perhaps it's the other way around. Either way it's wrong.

This fixation on everything international from the cult of Common Core is starting to make sense. Perhaps Arne Duncan just happens to agree with UNESCO, and its Agenda 21, and sees it as an honorable alliance to make between our country and the world.

Perhaps he thinks the United States should acknowledge that it is just like every other country in the world, and that we should band together with them to have common educational standards? Perhaps he believes in a world Common Core?

Only Arne knows. At least he is, like most Common Core cultists, consistently not being clear about his true intentions. So let's give him points for that. Using Common Core math, I'll give him three circles and a triangle of points. He can figure that one out.

Did you think that we could talk about the global cult of Common Core without mentioning Bill Gates? Bill Gates was also lurking around in the shadows at UNESCO with his fanny pack on, scheming towards getting in on the action. In 2004, Bill Gates signed an agreement of cooperation with UNESCO where Microsoft would develop programs to integrate technology into education and community programs to support UNESCO's sustainability goals worldwide. Bill Gates initialed every page of the document of cooperation and reaffirmed his support of UNESCO's objectives and program goals, which include its World Board of Education role in promoting Agenda 21 and transforming our children's minds toward sustainability. The link to this document is in the notes section. Bill Gates, of course, gives loads of money to UNESCO to promote its agenda according to his foundation's webpage. Bill Gates always wants a return on his investment. You have to wonder if the World Board of Education will make Microsoft the exclusive informational technology company for their sustainability education efforts.

Again, Bill Gates tends to show his intentions with regards to the Common Core (the American cult and the World cult). Arne Duncan and the Common Core crowd, on the other hand, are always putting forth their Common Core cover story, while their actions tell a different story. Maya Angelou has remarked, "The first time someone shows you who they are, believe them." We know who you are, Arne Duncan.

9

A Very American Story

"The eyes of the world are upon you. And if they see you repudiate your past, abandon that which has brought you to greatness, become just another country, they, too, will have lost something" Daniel Hannan, <u>*The New Road to Serfdom*</u>

My journey began over a year ago with a something's-not-right sort of feeling I had while working with the Common Core technocrats on their Common Core test in Chicago. That feeling caused me to research and gather facts with which I would eventually formulate my opposition to the Common Core.

As events related to the Common Core played out in the media, and while working on yet another Common Core test group in Chicago, I began to feel an upsurge of urgency. It was an urgency to share my knowledge with parents. I was reticent to make my opposition to the Common Core public. Then I began to see groups of concerned *Mama Grizzlies* and *Bad-ass Mothers* around the country being dismissed and maligned for their concerns about the Common Core.

It was a small band of those *Bad-ass Mothers* in Tucson, Arizona, that gave me the inspiration to finally speak out against the cult of Common Core. A group of moms in the *Amphitheater School District* rose up against their district's implementation of the

Common Core at a school board meeting. They were raising all the questions and concerns that I had had about the Common Core.

They were dismissed as ill-informed by some, but I knew that they actually had all their facts correct. They were maligned as a vocal minority, when I knew that they spoke for many of us teachers who were a silent majority. Their fearlessness pushed me to begin advocating for the removal of the Common Core from our state by using facts and real life experiences garnered from the classroom and from working with the Common Core cultists on the Common Core test.

The cult of Common Core would invite me to work on their PARCC test four more times. Each time I declined. The PARCC item review groups were always scheduled to take place during the school week and would require a teacher to miss a week of school each time. How any teacher would take 5 weeks off from their students in their classroom to work on a test is beyond me. Most of the teachers I worked with in Chicago felt the same. I'm sure the cult of Common Core will replace us with other teachers to serve as window dressing. Besides, I began to feel as if I was contributing towards the success of the beast. I am now in the fight against this beast, this cult of Common Core, and it feels right. I'm not sure of what may occur as I speak out against the Common Core, my governor, and my Superintendent of Education, who are pushing it. But it is time to do what is right, and the right outcome will occur. I am now in the fight. I hope you find this book a reliable source of information and ammunition for your fight against the Common Core, your fight for the minds of our children, and your fight for our country's exceptionalism.

The cult of Common Core has billions of dollars, but our side has the passion and the commitment to fight on behalf of our children. The cult of Common Core has sounded the alarm and is releasing their flying monkeys in a last ditch effort to squelch the anti-Common Core forces multiplying across the nation.

Just as our ill-equipped, ragtag militias defeated the biggest, most well equipped militaries in the world, in the War for Independence, so too shall we defeat this leviathan called the Common Core. It is a very American story and I have a feeling that it will be written by a coalition of *Mama Grizzlies* and *Bad-ass Mothers!*

Appendix A

The members of the Standards Development Work Group released by the National Governors Association (NGA) in 2009. There is no information as to who chose these group members or the criteria that was used.

Math Standards Group

1. Sara Clough, ACT (testing co)

2. Phil Daro, America's Choice (textbook co)

3. Susan K. Eddins, Educational Consultant

4. Kaye Forgione, Achieve (Common Core)

5. John Kraman, Achieve

6. Marci Ladd, College Board (testing co)

7. William McCallum, Achieve

8. Sherri Miller, ACT

9. Ken Mullen, ACT

10. Robin O'Callaghan, College Board

11. Andrew Schwartz, College Board

12. Laura McGiffert Slover, Achieve

13. Douglas Sovde, Achieve

14. Natasha Vasavada, College Board

15. Jason Zimba, Student Achievement Partners(Comm Core)

English Language Arts Standards Work Group

1. Sara Clough, ACT

2. David Coleman, Student Achievement Partners

3. Sally Hampton, America's Choice

4. Joel Harris, College Board

5. Beth Hart, College Board

6. John Kraman, Achieve

7. Laura McGiffert Slover, Achieve

8. Nina Metzner, ACT

9. Sherri Miller, ACT

10. Sandy Murphy, Professor, UC-Davis

11. Jim Patterson, ACT

12. Sue Pimentel, Achieve

13. Natasha Vasavada, College Board

14. Martha Vockley, Founder, VockleyLang, LLC

   (Educational Consultant)

Appendix B

Grants given by Bill Gates to support the implementation of the Common Core in 2013 alone. This was taken from the Bill & Melinda Gates Foundation grant website. Bill Gates has given a total of $2.3 billion toward the Common Core to date, according to GA State Professor, Jack Hassard.

1. Committee for Economic Development 2013 Global Policy & Advocacy US Program $865,593

2. National Conference of State Legislatures 2013 Global Policy & Advocacy US Program $557,046

3. Bellwether Education Partners, Inc. 2013 College-Ready US Program $1,981,978

4. The Aspen Institute Inc 2013 College-Ready US Program $1,500,003

5. Motion Math, Inc. 2013 College-Ready US Program $100,000

6. National Indian Education Association 2013 Global Policy & Advocacy US Program $600,000

7. Center for American Progress 2013 College-Ready US Program $550,000

8. Southeast Asia Resource Action Center 2013 Global Policy & Advocacy US Program $440,035

9. Foundation for Excellence in Education Inc. 2013 College-Ready US Program $2,000,000

10. The NEA Foundation for the Improvement of Education 2013 College-Ready US Program $501,580

11. Achievement First Inc. 2013 College-Ready US Program $837,355

12. Americas Promise-The Alliance For Youth 2013 College-Ready US Program $100,001

13. Policy Innovators In Education Network, Inc. 2013 College-Ready US Program $499,951

14. James B. Hunt, Jr. Institute for Educational Leadership and Policy Foundation, Inc. 2013 College-Ready US Program $1,749,070

15. New Venture Fund 2013 College-Ready US Program $3,213,686

16. Tennessee State Collaborative on Reforming Education 2013 College-Ready US Program $250,000

17. Summit Public Schools 2013 College-Ready US Program $250,000

18. Military Child Education Coalition 2013 College-Ready US Program $563,611

19. Learning Matters, Inc. 2013 College-Ready US Program $25,000

20. Aspire Public Schools 2013 College-Ready US Program $249,855

21. Rockefeller Philanthropy Advisors, Inc. 2013 College-Ready US Program $2,500,000

22. Research for Action Inc 2013 College-Ready US Program $650,000

23. National Catholic Educational Association 2013 College-Ready US Program $100,007

24. National Governors Association Center For Best Practices 2013 College-Ready US Program $750,000

25. Regents University Of California Los Angeles 2013 College-Ready US Program $942,527

26. Education Development Center, Inc. 2013 College-Ready US Program $211,795

27. James B. Hunt, Jr. Institute for Educational Leadership and Policy Foundation, Inc. 2013 College-Ready US Program $500,000

28. University of Missouri – Columbia 2013 College-Ready US Program $249,826

29. Massachusetts Institute of Technology 2013 College-Ready US Program $115,000

30. The Achievement Network 2013 College-Ready US Program $250,249

31. University of Florida 2013 College-Ready US Program $250,000

32. Region 8 ESC of Northeast Indiana 2013 College-Ready US Program $249,505

33. Center for Applied Linguistics 2013 College-Ready US Program $249,396

34. KnowledgeWorks Foundation 2013 College-Ready US Program $241,747

35. DePaul University 2013 College-Ready US Program $248,343

36. Perkins School for the Blind 2013 College-Ready US Program $249,113

37. ConnectEDU, Inc. 2013 College-Ready US Program $499,375

38. Puget Sound Educational Service District 2013 College-Ready US Program $247,465

39. Expeditionary Learning Outward Bound, Inc. 2013 College-Ready US Program $250,000

40. National Math and Science Initiative Inc. 2013 College-Ready US Program $248,760

41. National Center for Family Literacy Inc. 2013 College-Ready US Program $239,796

42. Association for Supervision and Curriculum Development 2013 College-Ready US Program $244,733

43. Arkansas Public School Resource Center Inc 2013 College-Ready US Program $200,000

44. Facing History and Ourselves National Foundation, Inc. 2013 College-Ready US Program $231,846

45. Battelle For Kids 2013 College-Ready US Program $249,808

46. Center for Teaching Quality, Inc. 2013 College-Ready US Program $249,471

47. New Visions for Public Schools, Inc 2013 College-Ready US Program $250,000

48. National Council of Teachers of English 2013 College-Ready US Program $249,482

49. New Teacher Center 2013 College-Ready US Program $250,000

50. The George Washington University 2013 College-Ready US Program $259,895

51. Harvard University 2013 College-Ready US Program $557,168

52. Council for a Strong America 2013 College-Ready US Program $1,550,000

53. American Agora Foundation Inc 2013 College-Ready US Program $100,000

54. The NEA Foundation for the Improvement of Education 2013 College-Ready US Program $3,882,600 (Union)

55. Council of Chief State School Officers 2013 College-Ready US Program $4,000,000

56. iCivics, Inc. 2013 College-Ready US Program $500,000

57. Benchmark Education Company LLC 2013 College-Ready US Program $25,000

58. Six Red Marbles LLC 2013 College-Ready US Program $500,000

59. LearnZillion, Inc. 2013 College-Ready US Program $250,000

60. Common Ground Software Inc. 2013 College-Ready US Program $500,000

61. Filament Games, LLC 2013 College-Ready US Program $25,000

62. University of Washington Foundation 2013 College-Ready US Program $610,819

63. Council of Chief State School Officers 2013 College-Ready US Program $799,825

64. National Association of State Boards of Education 2013 College-Ready US Program $800,000

65. New Venture Fund 2013 College-Ready US Program $1,150,000

66. New America Foundation 2013 College-Ready US Program $200,002

67. National Congress of Parents and Teachers 2013 College-Ready US Program $499,962

68. The Aspen Institute Inc 2013 College-Ready US Program $74,290

69. Pennsylvania Partnerships for Children 2013 Global Policy & Advocacy US Program $240,000

70. WestEd 2013 College-Ready US Program $30,000

71. Michigan State University 2013 College-Ready US Program $650,000

72. LearnZillion, Inc. 2013 College-Ready US Program $965,525

73. University of Kentucky Research Foundation 2013 College-Ready US Program $1,000,000

74. Delaware Department of Education 2013 College-Ready US Program $400,000

75. National Paideia Center Inc 2013 College-Ready US Program $659,788

76. The Aspen Institute Inc 2013 College-Ready US Program $3,615,655

More detailed information on a few of the grantees

1. Council of Chief State School Officers
Date: July 2013
Purpose: to support the development of high quality assessments to measure the Common Core State Standards
Amount: $4,000,000

2. Bellwether Education Partners, Inc.
Date: November 2013
Purpose: to support CoreSpring, an initiative to build a bank of shared Common Core aligned formative item and

assessment resources that assure improved discoverability, availability and interoperability
Amount: $1,981,978

3. Foundation for Excellence in Education Inc.
Date: October 2013
Purpose: to support an outreach and public information project that builds support and understanding of the Common Core State Standards and aligned assessments in states
Amount: $2,000,000

4. New Venture Fund
Date: October 2013
Purpose: to support successful implementation of the Common Core State Standards by building public awareness and understanding
Amount: $3,213,686

5. The Aspen Institute
Date: October 2013
Purpose: to support a group of school district leaders in their efforts to implement the Common Core standards
Amount: $1,500,003

6. James B. Hunt Jr. Institute for Educational Leadership and Policy Foundation, Inc.
Date: October 2013
Purpose: to support states in their continued implementation of the Common Core State Standards
Amount: $1,749,070

7. Council for a Strong America
Date: July 2013

Purpose: to educate and engage stakeholders about the Common Core and teacher development through a range of communications activities
Amount: $1,550,000

8. National Association of State Boards of Education
Date: June 2013
Purpose: to support a development plan for the organization and its efforts to provide training and information to implement Common Core State Standards

Amount: $800,000

Appendix C

Questions When Challenging the cult of Common Core

The following questions were taken from the Common Core: Education Without Representation website. They are excellent questions to be asked when confronting the cult of Common Core.

http://whatiscommoncore.wordpress.com/tag/james-milgram/

1. Is Common Core constitutional? Why or why not?

2. How important is the defense of **local autonomy and local control of schools**, to you personally –and does Common Core affect local control in any way? **Yes or no?**

3. The Common Core itself calls itself a "living work" and it admits that the document will change. Does the State School Board have authority over the copyrighted Common Core "document" to change the document itself? (To clarify: this is not a question of adding 15% as the Common Core governance allows a state to add in-state, but we are asking about changing the national standards themselves.) **Yes or No?**

4. Can **voters** remove from positions of power the people who hold copyright over their state's Common Core standards (Board of Directors of CCSSO/NGA) if we do not approve of the direction of Common Core? **Yes or No?**

5. Are those who hold copyright over Common Core subject to transparency ("sunshine" laws) –so that the our state board of education can supervise the decisions which affect and govern us? **Yes or No?**

6. **Where** can I read for myself how the states-led (inter-state) **amendment process** will work when we want to change something in the Common Core standards, if a process exists?

7. Where can I see for myself the evidence that Common Core standards have been **field tested prior to implementation**, so they were proven to be of superior academic quality, if testing evidence exists?

8. Professor Christopher Tienken of Seton Hall University has called Common Core "**educational malpractice**." Regardless of how you feel about Common Core, **how would you recognize educational malpractice** if you saw it; what would be its hallmarks?

9. Would widespread mandating of experimental, untested standards constitute educational malpractice?

10. Where can I see for myself the specific countries and specific standards to which the Common Core standards are "internationally benchmarked" if such benchmarking exists?

11. Where is the American process of representation of individuals in the Common Core education and assessments system, if it exists?

12. Where can I see for myself empirical, researched evidence (not opinion) that Common Core's increasing informational text and decreasing classic literature will benefit children, if it exists?

13. Where can I see for myself empirical, researched evidence that Common Core's move away from traditional math toward constructivist math will benefit our children, if it exists?

14. Many mathematicians and math experts, even including Common Core architect and advocate Jason Zimba, have pointed out

that students who want to take Calculus in college will need to take more math than Common Core math courses in high school. What should the Utah State School Board do to make sure Utah students are truly prepared for STEM careers despite Common Core's low math standards?

15. A mathematician is one who has an advanced degree in advanced mathematics; a math educator is one who has an advanced degree in educating students on any level of math. How do you feel about the fact that there was only one actual mathematician on the Common Core validation committee, Dr. James Milgram, and that he refused to sign off because he said the standards were not legitimate math for college preparation?

16. Several official documents show that there is a 15% cap on a state adding to the Core; we also from Common Core architect Jason Zimba and validation committee member James Milgram that Common Core math does not prepare students for STEM math careers; then how are our students to prepare for STEM careers?

17. If local students break through the common core academic ceiling and add more than the allowable 15% to their local standards, how will that 15% be taught using common core aligned math and English tests and texts?

18. Although we have been told that Common Core was state-led, no citizen in this state received an invitation to discuss this, before math and English standards were decided. To make sure **this does not happen again**, please explain the vetting process for teachers and parents, before we add upcoming national science, national social studies, and national sex ed standards.

19. Which element played a larger role in states's decision to adopt Common Core: the chance to win Race to the Top grant money, or a thorough review of the Common Core academically? Please give evidence for your answer.

20. Where can I read our state's cost analysis for implementing Common Core standards, tests and professional development costs?

21. Does the Common Core essentially discriminate against talents and interests that are not consistent with their prescribed knowledge and skills?

22. What roles does the State Longitudinal Database System (SLDS)play in reporting to the <u>federal Edfacts Exchange</u> and to the national E.I.M.A.C./CCSSO data collection machines?

23. How do you respond to the question asked by Christopher Tienken of Seton Hall University? He said:
"This is not data-driven decision making… Yet this nation will base the future of its entire public education system, and its children, upon this lack of evidence. Where is the evidence to support the rhetoric surrounding the Common Core standards?"

24. Do you see Common Core's emphasis on testing as potentially harming American creativity and entrepreneurial fields in which U.S. graduate have historically led the world– or do you see this emphasis on standardization and testing as simply creating more individuals who are very good at taking tests– like students in some Asian countries– without any harm being done to creativity or love of learning?

25. The Constitution assigns education to the states, not to the federal government. Also, the federal General Educational Provisons Act (GEPA) states: "No provision of any applicable program shall be construed to authorize any department, agency, officer, or employee of the United States to exercise any direction, supervision, or control over the curriculum, program of instruction, administration, or personnel of any educational institution, school, or school system …" In light of this, please explain why our state has <u>partnered with </u>those who agree to micromanagement by the federal department of education such as the CCSSO.

26. Which portions of local autonomy have been traded for federally-lauded Common Core standards and tests?

27. What types of legal protections does student data have in writing that can protect us from the federal government and vendors and

researchers– in light of recent changes to FERPA privacy regulations, and in light of the federally funded and federally-reporting State Longitudinal Database System (SLDS) that is partnered with the CCSSO (and PESC) under our state's SLDS grant agreement?

28. For students in the United States to be globally competitive, they must offer something different, that is, something that cannot be obtained at a lower cost in developing countries. High test scores in a few subjects can be achieved in most developing countries, so how could Common Core increase global competitiveness for U.S. students?

30. How can any test predict global competiveness or economic growth?

31. What empirical evidence do you have that high Common Core test scores could result in higher levels of innovation, creativity, and entrepreneurship?

32. If countries like Estonia, Hungary, Slovenia, Vietnam, Latvia, and Poland routinely outscore the U.S. on standardized tests such as PISA, why isn't their per capita gross domestic product or other personal economic indicators equal to those in the U.S. (World Bank, 2013)? In other words, what evidence do we have that pressuring students to focus on standardized testing will improve the U.S. economy?

33. Are you aware, that when you disaggregate the data by percentages of poverty in a school, the U.S. scores at the top of all the international PISA tests? (see Riddle, 2009) In other words, why are we pushing Common Core when our previous system of local control and freedom worked better academically than other countries' governmentally standardized systems?

34. Companies like Boeing and GE are allowed to give their technology, utility patents, and know-how to the Chinese in return for being able to sell their products in China (Prestowitz, 2012). Can U.S. emphasis on standardized test scores create global

competitiveness, really, or is it more likely that we should change the policy of allowing U.S. multinationals to give away our technological advantages, to increase our global competitiveness?

35. Are you aware that 81% of U.S. engineers are qualified to work in multinational corporations – the highest percentage in the world (Kiwana, 2012) while only 10% of Chinese engineering graduates and 25% of Indian engineers are prepared to work in multinational corporations or corporations outside of China or India (Gereffi, et al., 2006; Kiwana, 2012)?

36. Are you aware that the U.S. produces the largest numbers of utility patents (innovation patents) per year and has produced over 100,000 a year for at least the last 45 years under our previous system? How will Common Core better this accomplishment?

Notes

Preface

1. Common Core not "state led". Stimulus money tied to changing education policies(Race to the Top Announcement) http://www2.ed.gov/news/pressreleases/2009/07/07242009.html
2. An example of one governor, AZ's Jan Brewer, agreeing to adopt the Common Core standards, test, and data gathering structure- Race To the Top Application (p.21-22) http://www2.ed.gov/programs/racetothetop/phase2-applications/arizona.pdf

Chapter 1

3. Teacher performance evaluations to be connected to Common Core test scores. "Race to Top Winners Feel Heat on Teacher Evaluations" by Sean Cavanagh, Education Week, 2/2011. http://www.edweek.org/ew/articles/2011/09/14/03evaluation_ep.h31.html?tkn=ROUFos5Qop0wqLv7yduXFqVyj%2BJpo%2B4EEmYv&cmp=ENL-TU-NEWS2

4. Opposition to standards comes from the Left and Right. "Common Core Curriculum Now Has Critics on the Left" by Al Baker, New York Times, 2/2014. http://www.nytimes.com/2014/02/17/nyregion/new-york-early-champion-of-common-core-standards-joins-critics.html?_r=2

Chapter 2

5. Progressives are at odds with America's founding principles. "Glenn Beck, Progressives and Me" Ronald Pestritto, author of Woodrow Wilson and the Roots of Modern Liberalism, 2005, Hillsdale College Professor. Wall Street Journal, 9/2010. http://online.wsj.com/news/articles/SB10001424052748704554104575435942829722602?mg=reno64wsj&url=http%3A%2F%2Fonline.wsj.com%2Farticle%2FSB10001424052748704554104575435942829722602.html

6. David Coleman is a key architect of Common Core. http://www.nga.org/cms/home/news-room/news-releases/page_2009/col2-content/main-content-list/title_common-core-state-standards-development-work-group-and-feedback-group-announced.html

7. David Coleman becomes head of College Board – will align to Common Core http://press.collegeboard.org/releases/2012/college-board-names-david-coleman-new-president

8. College Board to promote Social Justice agenda program Access to Rigour http://www.breitbart.com/Big-Government/2014/03/10/With-Common-Core-in-Trouble-Obama-s-Social-Justice-Education-Agenda-To-Be-Achieved-With-New-Dumbed-Down-SAT

9. Changes to dumb down SAT to align with Common Core http://www.theblaze.com/stories/2014/03/05/they-just-announced-major-changes-to-the-satand-theres-a-tie-to-common-core/

10. Arne Duncan calls opposition to Common Core mostly "white suburban" moms who discover their kids are not as brilliant as they thought they were.

http://www.washingtonpost.com/blogs/answer-sheet/wp/2013/11/16/arne-duncan-white-surburban-moms-upset-that-common-core-shows-their-kids-arent-brilliant/

11. Brewer changes name of Common Core in AZ to AZ College and Career Readiness Standards
http://azstarnet.com/news/local/education/common-core-name-changes-standards-remain/article_7a97e40c-bdbf-579f-960c-cbad2db9e9c4.html

12. Common Core backed Teacher of the Year Program to push Common Core.
http://achieve.org/search/node/teachers%20of%20the%20year

13. Copyright for Common Core Standards belongs to Natl Governor's Association and CCSSO
http://www.corestandards.org/public-license

14. Teachers of the Year is a project of the CCSSO – Common Core group that wrote and own copyright for the common core standards.
http://www.ccsso.org/Resources/Programs/National_Teacher_of_the_Year_Program.html

15. Teacher advocates for Common Core-Teacher Voices Convening (TVC)-being trained with Gates money.
http://news.heartland.org/newspaper-article/2014/01/28/foundations-spend-millions-promoting-common-core

Chapter 3

16. Elementary and Secondary Education Act 1965-no national curriculum may be mandated
http://www2.ed.gov/legislation/FedRegister/other/2008-4/101708a.html

17. Phyllis Schlafly points out that the 1965 Elementary and Secondary Education Act, the 1970 General Education Provisions Act and the 1979 law establishing the U.S. Department of Education all prohibit a national curriculum http://www.theblaze.com/stories/2014/02/28/is-common-core-the-one-policy-the-public-wont-let-obama-administration-get-away-with/

18. Common Core not "state led". Stimulus money tied to changing education policies(Race to the Top Announcement) http://www2.ed.gov/news/pressreleases/2009/07/07242009.html

19. An example of one governor, AZ's Jan Brewer, agreeing to adopt the Common Core standards, test, and data gathering structure- Race To the Top Application (p.21-22) http://www2.ed.gov/programs/racetothetop/phase2-applications/arizona.pdf

20. National Governors Association (NGA) www.nga.org

21. Council of Chief State School Officers http://www.ccsso.org/

22. States agree to adopt 85% of Common Core Standards(not open to be changed), states have input on only 15% of its standards(see p.5) Overview of history of tests and standards. http://www.k12center.org/rsc/pdf/Coming_Together_April_2012_Final.PDF

23. (PARCC) Partnership for Assessment of Readiness for College and Career http://www.parcconline.org/about-parcc

24. SBAC (Smarter Balanced Assessment Consortium) http://www.smarterbalanced.org/ www.smarterbalanced.org/resources-events/faqs (fed grant info)

Chapter 4

25. Data Suctioning systems (SLDS) defined. Recommended changes to FERPA regulations defined.
http://www.hslda.org/commoncore/Topic10.aspx
http://epic.org/apa/ferpa/default.html

26. Changes to FERPA in letter from US Dept of Education
http://www2.ed.gov/policy/gen/guid/fpco/pdf/pprasuper.pdf

27. Big Data salivates over data gathering possibilities."Promoting Grit, Tenacity, and Perseverance: Critical Factors for Success in the 21st Century" (U.S. Department of Education, February 2013),
http://www.ed.gov/edblogs/technology/files/2013/02/OET-Draft-Grit-Report-2-17-13.pdf

28. "New York Parents Furious at Program, Inbloom, That Compiles Private Student Information for Companies That Contract with It to Create Teaching Tools," New York Daily News, March 13, 2013, accessed June 18, 2013, http://www.nydailynews.com/new-york/student-data-compiling-system-outrages-article-1.1287990?pgno=1

29. Gov LePage ME Executive order against sharing student data
http://truthinamericaneducation.com/common-core-state-standards/maine-governor-signs-executive-order-protecting-local-control-student-privacy/

30. List of 2013 Gates Foundation grant recipients
http://www.washingtonpost.com/blogs/answer-sheet/wp/2013/11/27/gates-foundation-pours-millions-into-common-core-in-2013/

31. Gates has given $2.3 billion to date pushing Common Core
http://www.artofteachingscience.org/why-bill-gates-defends-the-common-core/

32. Gates at SXSW Conference. Sees $9.2 billion market in k-12
http://www.fastcompany.com/3006708/creative-conversations/bill-gates-gives-sxsw-education-conference-keynote-cites-9-billion-ti

33. Gates on TED Talks Education. Talks technology and cameras in classroom.
http://www.bing.com/videos/search?q=TED+talks+education+bill+gates&FORM=VIRE7#view=detail&mid=A9731316B4A86E116039A9731316B4A86E116039

34. College Blackout Study: Bill Gates wants to continue to track through college and beyond using the Student Unit Record System
http://www.insidehighered.com/sites/default/server_files/files/CollegeBlackout_March10_Noon.pdf

35. Gates gave US Chamber of Commerce 1.3 Million to promote the CC in 2013
http://www.breitbart.com/Big-Government/2014/02/15/Are-Americans-Rejecting-Academic-Standards-or-One-Size-Fits-All-Nationalized-Standards

36. Bill Coleman uses Organizing for America data gurus to identify Hispanic kids using data systems
http://www.breitbart.com/Big-Government/2014/02/02/Obama-s-Re-Election-Team-Invited-By-Common-Core-Architect-David-Coleman-To-Collect-Student-Data-On-Poor-and-Latino-Low-Hanging-Fruit

37. Obama 2015 budget earmarks millions for Common Core data suctioning and social justice programs.
http://www.ed.gov/news/press-releases/obama-administration-2015-budget-prioritizes-key-education-investments-provide-o

38. Regulatory changes to FERPA laws(3/2011) by Dept of Ed allowing sharing of student data without parent notification to include contractors advising schools and assessment groups (Common Core)..” to organizations conducting studies for or on behalf of the school making the disclosure for the purposes of

administering predictive tests, administering student aid
programs, or improving instruction;"
http://www2.ed.gov/policy/gen/guid/fpco/ferpa/parents.html

39. Coming Together for Achievement:US Dept of Ed commissioned
report states that PARCC and SBAC testing groups each got $175
million to develop tests (p.15) and tells teachers how tit should be
implemented in classroom (p.8-10) or curriculum and provides
exemplars.
http://www.k12center.org/rsc/pdf/Coming_Together_April_2012
_Final.PDF

Chapter 5

(much of Bill Gates ' information has been annotated above)

40. Gates admits teachers will align curriculum to the test and data
mining. Pat Gray, the Blaze.
http://www.theblaze.com/contributions/arne-duncan-youre-a-
liar-common-core-will-destroy-american-education/

Chapter 6

41. GE-list of grants handed out includes Student Achievement
Partners (Bill Coleman/Jason Zimba's company) $18 million. Many
of the grantees mimic the Gates Foundation grantees.
http://www.gefoundation.com/developing-futures-in-
education/partners/

42. Bill Ayers wrote the Chicago Annenberg Challenge Application .
http://sonatabio.com/CAC/CAC-application.pdf

43. Stanley Kurtz-National Review Online-definitive article on
Obama/Ayers connection and the Annenberg challenge in
Chicago.
http://online.wsj.com/news/articles/SB122212856075765367

44. Annenberg Challenge had no real effect on Chicago schools. Coleman/Zimba negotiate $2.3 million deal with Arne Duncan, CEO of Chicago Schools to package data w/Grow Network. http://www.educationviews.org/common-core-architect-david-coleman/ Danette Clark,EdNews

Chapter 7

45. Fordham Institute Study (2010)found 13 state standards were at par or better than the Common Core and 3 states had standards superior to them http://edexcellencemedia.net/publications/2010/201007_state_education_standards_common_standards/Arizona.pdf

46. Dr. James Milgram math expert refused to validate Common Core, says it is subpar when compared internationally and puts our kids at least 2 yrs behind in math. http://www.foxnews.com/opinion/2013/07/30/do-math-common-core-massive-risky-experiment-on-your-kids/

47. NGA releases list of authors of common core standards. No k-12 teachers on writing group. The proceedings "of the group will remain confidential". http://www.nga.org/cms/home/news-room/news-releases/page_2009/col2-content/main-content-list/title_common-core-state-standards-development-work-group-and-feedback-group-announced.html

48. Testing companies use students to field test PARCC/SBAC test, stand to make millions. http://michellemalkin.com/2014/03/19/revolt-against-the-testing-tyrants/ (Michelle Malkin)

49. PISA test broken down by ethnicity-U.S. kids do really well. http://www.vdare.com/articles/pisa-scores-show-demography-is-destiny-in-education-too-but-washington-doesnt-want-you-to-k

50. Big Business, Chamber of Commerce, Jeb Bush dumping millions into Common Core ad blitz
http://michellemalkin.com/2014/03/21/get-to-know-the-common-core-marketing-overlords/

51. Latest legislation to end involvement in Common Core by Truth in American Education.
http://truthinamericaneducation.com/common-core-state-standards/2014-common-core-legislation-round-up/

52. The National Hispanic Christian Leadership Conference endorses Common Core as the Common Core announces new initiatives channeling millions to Hispanics.
http://hispanicevangelical.org/

53. Brookings Institute study finds no difference in academic improvement between Common Core adopted states and those that never adopted the standards (AK, TX, VA, NE).
http://www.breitbart.com/Big-Government/2014/03/21/Study-Common-Core-Standards-Will-Have-Little-To-No-Impact-On-Student-Achievement

54. Dr. Sandra Stotsky, renowned standards expert refused to validate Common Core Standards.
http://www.breitbart.com/Big-Government/2014/01/14/Expert-Dr-Sandra-Stotsky-On-Common-Core-We-Are-A-Very-Naive-People

55. Truth in American Education
http://truthinamericaneducation.com/

56. Breitbart News   http://www.breitbart.com/big-government

57. The Blaze, Glenn Beck   http://www.theblaze.com/

58. Michelle Malkin   http://michellemalkin.com/

59. Phyllis Schlafly reports on Gates/UNESCO connectionhttp://www.crossroad.to/articles2/0013/common-core/bill_gates_teams_up_with_unesco.htm

60. UNESCO Document explaining role in Agenda 21 in education/teacher training. http://portal.unesco.org/en/ev.php-URL_ID=5434&URL_DO=DO_TOPIC&URL_SECTION=201.html

61. Jason Zimba says Common Core math will not prepare kids for high tech jobs and selective universities. US News, the Hechinger Report.http://www.usnews.com/news/special-reports/articles/2014/02/25/the-common-core-math-standards-content-and-controversy

62. Arne Duncan addresses the U.N.'s UNESCO to talk about education reform in the U.S.http://www.ed.gov/news/speeches/vision-education-reform-united-states-secretary-arne-duncans-remarks-united-nations-ed

63. Arne Duncan addresses the Sustainability Education Summit 9/2010 and emphasizes sustainability education http://www.ed.gov/news/speeches/greening-department-education-secretary-duncans-remarks-sustainability-summit

64. Microsoft/UNESCO Cooperation Agreement http://www.eagleforum.org/links/UNESCO-MS.pdf

65. Common Core and Agenda 21, Alex Newman,The New American http://www.thenewamerican.com/culture/education/item/17930-common-core-and-un-agenda-21-mass-producing-green-global-serfs

CPSIA information can be obtained at www.ICGtesting.com
Printed in the USA
LVOW05s1841011014

406784LV00027B/1056/P

9 781497 456044